CAPONE'S CHICAGO

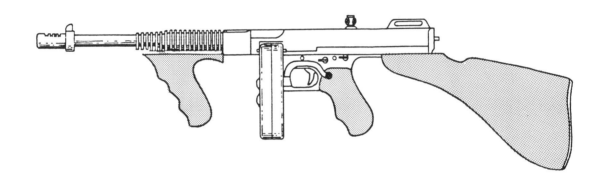

USM, Inc.
RAPID CITY, SD
57709-2600   USA
2000

United States Library of Congress Cataloging in Publication Data
USM, Inc.
International Standard Book Number (ISBN) 0-910667-13-6

Enright, Richard T., 19?? - 19??
Cowdery, Ray R., 1941-   , editor

Title: *Capone's Chicago!*
          10th American Edition

1.   HISTORY - Chicago; Capone; Gangsters; 1920s, Roaring Twenties
2.   CRIME - Gangsters; Chicago; 1920s, Roaring Twenties
3.   BIOGRAPHY - Capone, Alphonse

Printed in the United States of America

*Distributed exclusively
worldwide by:*

USM, Inc.
Post Office Box 2600
Rapid City, SD 57709-2600 USA
Fax: (605) 341-5488

*The checkered spine on this book was added to the new edition
in tribute to the heroic men and women of the Chicago Police.*

**Order additional copies of this book from your Internet or other bookseller.
If not available, write or fax USM at the address in the box above.**

INTRODUCTION

Chicago is a beautiful American city. It offers a never ending variety to the hundreds of thousands who visit the city each year. Its restaurants, architecture and lakeshore are world famous.

It was not always so. Chicago's industries, open spaces and four-seasons were an enormous magnet for 19th century Europeans looking for a home and opportunity. The frontier Chicago grew into a wonderful collection of ethnic neighborhoods -- Irish, Italian, Russian, Greek, German, Polish and others.

In many of the communities, making beer and liquor at home was as much a tradition as it was an effort to compete with licensed distileries and breweries. At least until 1920. With the enactment of the 18th Ammendment to the U.S. Constitution, it was no longer legal to manufacture or sell alcoholic beverages anywhere in this country for all practical purposes.

In spite of the law barring manufacture, the drinking of alcoholic beverages remained as popular as ever. The opportunity to profit from the manufacture, distribution and sale of alcohol was more than many Chicagoans could resist, so they enthusiastically got in the business. The opportunity to sell alcohol or to provide protection in various neighborhoods were valuable rights, and the competition for them was fierce.

It was not illegal in the 1920s to own a machine gun, so the "Chicago piano" quickly became one of the principal tools that gangs used to maintain their influence. The situation quickly deteriorated into open warfare. Hundreds of "soldiers" were killed on Chicago streets, in cars and at home, and the concept of being "taken for a ride" took on a new meaning. One man had more to do with this carnage than any other -- Al Capone.

This book was written in 1931 by Richard T. Enright and uniquely documents the bloodiest era in the history of Chicago.

Ray R. Cowdery
Northstar Maschek Books

Al Capone, Master Criminal

By Richard T. Enright

THE CLIMAX OF CAPONE'S BLOODY CAREER

"Only Capone kills like that," cried "Bugs" Moran when p o l i c e found the bodies of seven of his men lined up against a wall in the St. Valentine massacre. "They don't call that guy 'Bugs' for nothing," was Capone's comment.

CHAPTER ONE: Al Capone As I Know Him

AL CAPONE is a strange combination of the affable, g e n e r o u s smiling, handshaking, friendly Italian who likes to get his feet into carpet slippers and his heavy torso into a dressing gown, and the tense, hard-faced, frowning "gorilla man" with the livid scar on his left cheek bone.

I have seen him when it would be hardly possible to imagine him at anything more nearly criminal than shaking for smokes with a dice cup of a cigar stand.

I have seen him, aroused, when he moved like a panther springing for the kill.

He is about five feet, eight inches tall and weighs 190 pounds. Youth still looks out at you from his eyes which may bear a kindly, humorous glint or will flash black ferocity at a moment's notice. At this writing, I believe, he is not yet 34 years old.

There is still about him the mark of the army in which he served overseas during the World War. That great bulk of his is not all fat. Beneath lie great bulges of muscle that enable him at times to move with the speed and power of a tiger.

He loves music. I have seen tears in his eyes. His men watch the evidences of his emotional nature as do the intimates of a grand opera star.

His head is large and his neck is short which adds to the appearance of power that emanates from him. His eyebrows are black and bushy and his complexion is swarthy except where the scar that gave him his monicker cuts across his cheek.

There are legends about that scar. One is that he owes a German machine gunner for it, that he got it in a brush in the front line trenches in 1918. But the general belief is that he got it in the foray that resulted in his arrest for disorderly conduct in Olean, New York, before he ever saw Chicago.

The remarkable features of Capone's face are his eyes, it seems to me, for they have that faculty of seeing everything and of appearing to read the inmost thoughts of those upon whom they fall. Many a double-crosser in Al's organization has lost his poise when he stood before Capone in the gangster's headquarters in the old Metropole hotel.

7

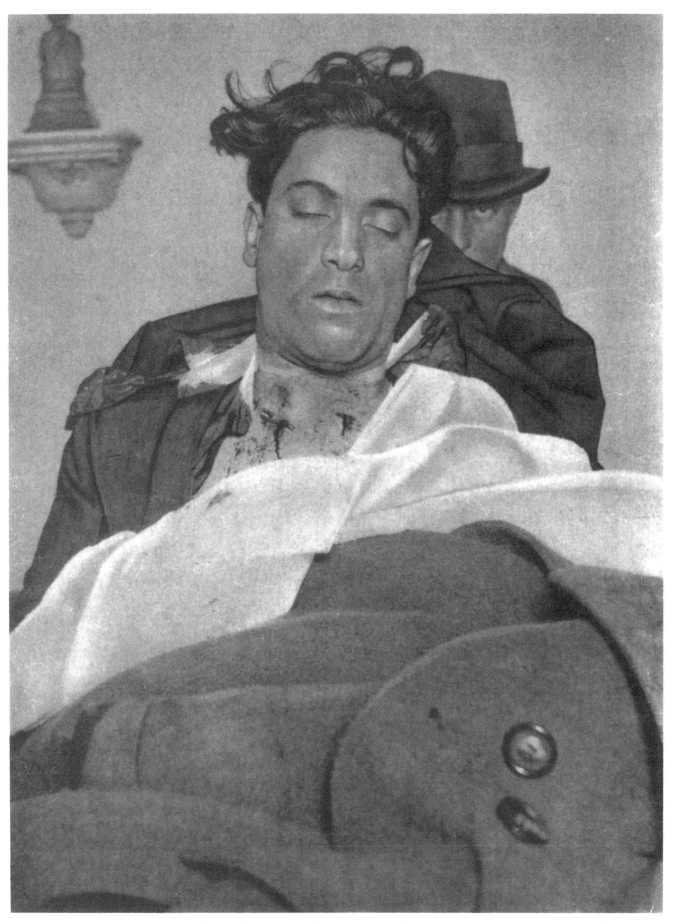

Frank Capone, brother of the Big Fellow, was killed in street fighting during the capture of Cicero, when gangsters terrorized voters and fought pistol battles with the police.

They are, moreover, the eyes of an actor for he can control them when he wishes so that those who look into them cannot know what goes on behind those bristling brows.

THE STRENGTH of Capone is his determination and that is not revealed by the thick, sometimes loose lips, the squat nose or the bullet head with its thick neck. It looks out of his eyes, however, and may be seen in the curve of his short, stubby fingers and powerful hands.

It must have taxed his tailor to dress this man but, like most gangsters, he is generally faultlessly costumed in public.

At least fifty and perhaps a hundred and fifty suits of clothes are in his wardrobe but I venture to say that not one of them is of conspicuous weave or of a cut that would attract attention except for its excellence.

For the most part his appearance is that of the perfectly groomed business man. His feet are small and always well shod, usually in black but sometimes with sport shoes that are noticeable. I have a feeling that Capone is vain of his feet.

His hats are of the finest quality and sit square on his head with a touch of curve to the brim but never with the tough swagger or the gangster's appearance of hiding under a tight pulled brim.

His eyes are so deep set that they need no shadowing.

I have never seen the Big Fellow with a pipe. He is often seen with a cigar. He smokes cigarets as do millions of young men since the war.

His collars and ties fit perfectly about the thick neck and even the neckties are seldom of an unusual pattern.

His overcoats mostly are black or dark and he shows a leaning toward the black velvet collar.

Ralph Capone, another brother of Al, is still one of the principal cogs in the Gangland Chief's deadly machine. He is shown here with his attorneys answering charges of falsifying income tax returns.

Frank Nitti, sometimes called The Enforcer, is said by some to be Capone's master killer. He holds the position of treasurer of Capone & Company. He is shown here being fingerprinted in Chicago.

IN HIS photographs, Capone usually turns the scarred left cheek away from the camera but even in front face pictures the scar has a way of disappearing under the photographic process so that it cannot always be detected.

It is not at all unusual for him to stand with a hand in his overcoat pocket or with a thumb hooked in his belt if he wears no overcoat. No doubt an automatic lies near his fingertips most of the time yet you have no impression that he is just ready to fire. I have seen a small gun peeping from a vest pocket but have never known him to make a threatening move with it.

Capone spends much time in dressing gown and slippers. This is probably due to the fact that there are many days in his life when he does not go out of his rooms and that he spends much of his time at home.

His life is not that of a physically active man and yet you have in his presence the impression of boundless physical energy. One of the reasons for this is that he has his own gymnasium where he keeps in fair condition most of the time.

That old quickness of movement is evident when he steps about a handball court. His hands are capable of giving a heavy thump to a punching bag and he knows what to do on a rowing machine.

He does not drive himself in the gymnasium as he does his men. Capone is insistent that his followers and especially his bodyguard keep in condition. His machine gun expert, Jack McGurn, once a professional boxer, puts on some pretty exhibitions with the bags occasionally and now and then there is a neat demonstration of the fistic art between a couple of the best glove men in the outfit.

Capone does not always wear a coat of mail beneath his well-fitting clothes. One reason for this is that his bodyguard is a dependable one and the discomforts of the bullet-proof vest are well known. Another reason is that gangland aims for the head now and this may be due to the popularity such armor once enjoyed.

I had almost said that gangland bullets go for the face these days but that isn't always true. More often the back of the head is the target for gangland does not face its victims as often as it sneaks up from behind.

WHEN AL went to jail in Philadelphia he wore a $50,000 diamond ring weighing 11½ carats. The diamond belt buckle he occasionally wears is also worth a small fortune as were those he gave to Jake Lingle and to several other of his friends. But the display of jewelry is by no means generally in evidence when Capone ventures forth. His underwear is always of the best materials but is not always silk.

In his office there are two pictures, one of George

Death's door has a new significance in gangland. Here is the body of Giuseppe Morello, kin of the "Artichoke King," Ciro Terranova, of New York. He was slain in a triple murder by gangmen, who poured a fusillade through the door.

Washington and one of William Hale Thompson. His desk is mahogany and of the latest design and equipment. He uses the French type of telephone and on the desk is a gold encrusted inkstand.

There is a handsome Chinese chest in his office and a cuckoo clock of extraordinary design.

Dr. Herbert M. Goddard of the Pennsylvania State Board of prison inspectors, operated on Capone while he was in Eastern Penitentiary, removing tonsils and adenoids. He sized up the personality of Capone in a few words just before Al's release there.

"I have never seen a prisoner more kind and cheery. He is accommodating. He does his work with a great deal of intelligence. He has brains."

He was particularly impressed with Capone's treatment and affection for his mother, his wife and his son, then about eleven.

When Capone travels in Chicago he goes in a limousine that is like an armored fort on wheels. Light cars ride ahead and behind and his passage through the loop lacks only the motorcycle outriders to be as elaborate at that of a visiting foreign general.

THE REALLY remarkable thing about Capone, the thing that gives him the high command of gangland is that he never breaks faith. His agreements with other gangsters have been kept till they themselves upset them by some overt act. His relations with his own men are such that few have attempted to double-cross him and those usually men who were not admitted to his inner councils.

Gangsters have been asked why Capone continues to live when thousands of dollars have been offered for his death. The answer is that his men are loyal to him, that he is surrounded by a group of lieutenants and guards upon whom he can depend as they depend on him for protection and support in everything they do.

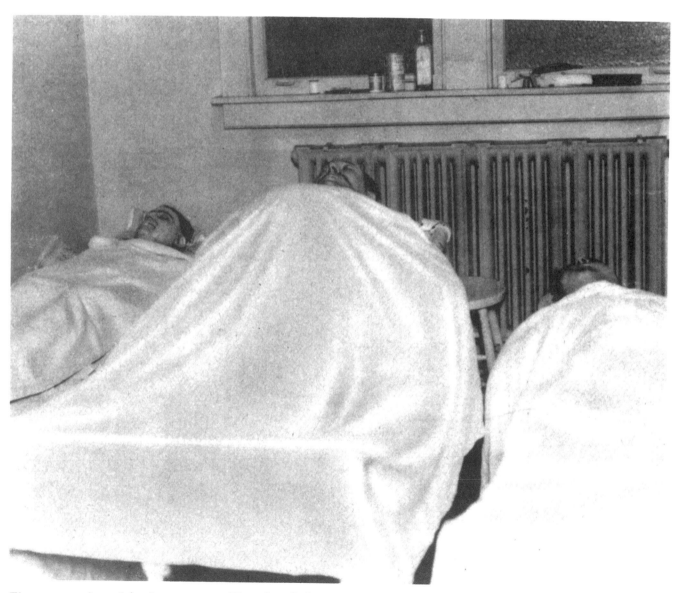

The gangster's end is the morgue. Here Joe Guinta, once president of the Unione Sicilione, and John Scalise and Albert Anselmi, sometimes called Capone's Homicide Squad, are seen after the testimonial banquet which ended with bullets.

When Al learns that he is suspected of a crime he seeks the office of the c o m m i s s i o n e r of detectives in Chicago and asks for a "show down". And they never have anything on Al. He is shown here with Commissioner John Stege.

Not content with shooting down Lorenzo Juliano, the killers ran his car over a cliff and left it a mass of wreckage with the dead body on a junk heap.

Breaks with Capone have been open breaks such as O'Banion's who became ambitious and declared war.

Those who have attempted to double-cross him have died with remarkable celerity and usually in dramatic fashion. Those who have declared war on him, with the exception of Bugs Moran, have usually passed out in similar fashion.

And yet, as you sit across his office desk with Al Capone or hold a fishing rod with him from the deck of his fishing boat, it is impossible to conceive of Al Capone planning these master killings.

To watch his infectious smile and the spread of his even teeth across it, to listen to the husky voice, to look at the hard muscled, callousless hand, is to doubt the evidence of a thousand accusations against this man.

When the mouth tightens, when the brows draw down and when the eyes spark with black anger as the blood rushes to the scar in his left cheek, it is easier to believe, but even then the cold, deadly ferocity that marks what are known as the Capone killings can hardly be accounted for.

You can imagine this man facing an enemy and shooting it out with him in armed conflict. You can imagine his stubby hands throttling a traitor in his ranks or smashing into the mouth as fists to halt a denunciation or a threat. You might even imagine him striking down a pistol arm and countering with the thrust of a long knife.

But you cannot picture Al Capone signing the death warrant of seven men in a St. Valentine's day massacre. You cannot picture him planning the glad-hand kill for Dion O'Banion or the banquet testimonial of death for Anselmi and Scalise.

"They've hung everything on me but the Chicago fire," Capone has said.

And in spite of all prejudices, in spite of preconceived notions, in spite of every evidence of your reason or your ears, you cannot, facing him, believe that he was guilty of cold-blooded death.

"How," you ask yourself, "can such a man as this bear the reputation of being the greatest criminal of all time?"

Yet this is his standing with the populace of the world today.

14

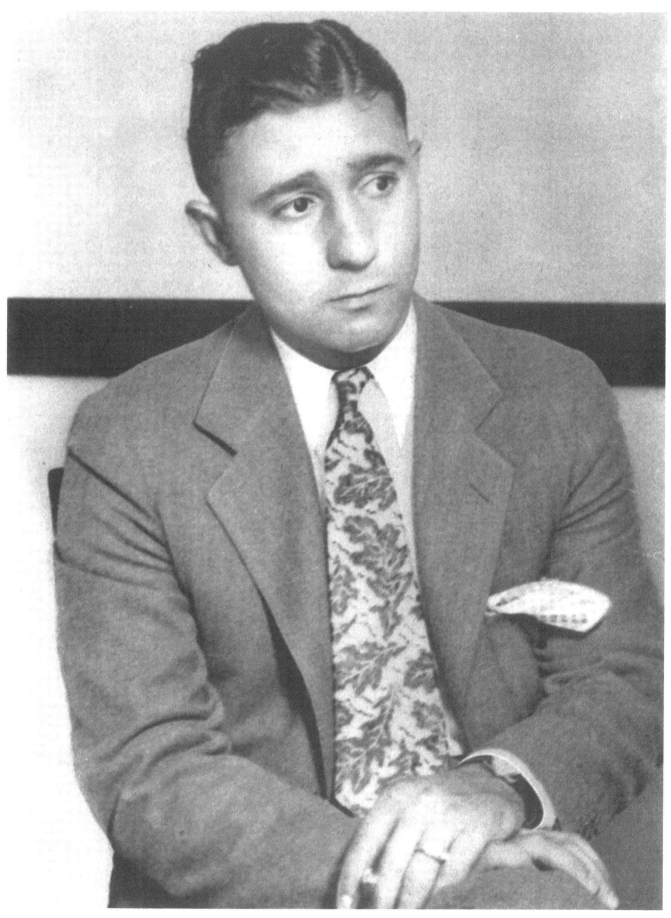

Capone's machine gun ace is Jack McGurn, who went gangster when his father was shot in the early beer battles in Chicago. He left the prize ring where he was making a name for himself and is said to have many notches on his machine gun.

No, Scarface Al is not drawing a gat! He was snapped while under arrest in Miami, Florida. His phalanx of high priced attorneys soon freed him of charges under Florida's vagrancy law.

CHAPTER TWO: The Emperor of Gangland

AL CAPONE is not dead—yet.

But Al lives every day with death and knows that it will get him in the end.

The world has put the finger on him. He is on the spot and—today, tomorrow, next week or next month, perhaps next year—sometime the gats will spit, the machine guns rattle, or the sawed-off shotguns roar.

And then the world and gangland will make holiday while the costliest coffin is borne behind the longest parade of flower-laden limousines and Al Capone will ride in the Last Parade.

There will be one floral piece missing from among those that have graced the biers of a hundred or two hundred or five hundred other gangsters. And that will be the great basket of costly flowers bearing the legend "From Al."

Scarface Al, as he used to be called before he rose to the ranks of the biggest of the Big Shots will not then ride down the street in his $20,000, seven-ton armored limousine with the bullet-proof glass windows. He will not then wear his bullet-proof vest.

Nor will he need those fourteen "torpedoes," who now guard him day and night.

Should these inevitable events occur speedily enough, the Big Shot will go to his marble mausoleum without having served a single minute in the bastilles of Illinois. For Al Capone has no police record as that term is ordinarily construed in Chicago.

So far as is known he has never served time anywhere but the ten months or so he spent in the Pennsylvania State penitentiary for carrying concealed weapons.

How this modern Napoleon of banditry rose to his present eminence as a man of untold wealth, ruling the underworld with the powers of an absolute monarch, whose headshake is a death sentence, until now he is even immune from the organized efforts of our own law and government—that is the tale you shall hear in all its unvarnished phases, in all its marvelous and bloody pageantry.

I am going to take you behind the scenes of gangdom and show you the man himself, in the flesh, with all his foibles and vanities, his cleverness, and his brutal indifference to death.

Jack Guzik, shown here whispering to his attorney, is said to be the brains of the Capone outfit and the organizer who put efficiency into the crime business. He was a former resort keeper.

Frank Rio, the mild looking man behind his attorney's shoulder, is Capone's chief bodyguard, the man who went to the penitentiary with the Chief when he took his sabbatical year behind the bars for carrying concealed weapons. Rio was booked on the same charge at the same time and served his term.

Let us glance first at a little clipping from a Chicago newspaper of 1922. In this item we first find mention of a man called "Al Caponi." In the item the reporter had the first name wrong, and spelled the last name "Caponi."

THAT was only nine years ago! Today Al's name has the stuff of headlines in it, and his income is enormous, running into the millions of dollars.

Only four years after that first mention of Al in the public prints, a United States District Attorney estimated that he operated on a gross of $70,000,000 a year in the illicit liquor business alone. In 1927 government officials estimated that he commanded a gross income of $105,000,000 a year from liquor interests and other rackets. Today his business is said to gross $300,000,000 a year.

Capone's standing army is estimated at five hundred killers.

Five hundred gangsters have died violent deaths since he came to Chicago but no man has ever brought forth the proof that Capone touched a trigger in one of them.

The most that can be said is that Capone's enemies died, that Capone's friends lived longer than the friends of other gangsters, that Capone's power, influence and income and the scope of his operations grew with the hammer blows of death.

It may be definitely stated that Capone's is the richest outlaw empire ever established in the history of the world. He commands resources greater than the greatest bandit chief in history. It is probable that his power is more nearly absolute than was that of the Emperor Nero. Napoleon was a piker compared with Capone.

And this whole vast empire has been built within nine years with no other implements than the six-gun made famous in the early history of America's great west.

He came to Chicago as a gunman. But there were many more who came the same way. What is it about Capone that has given him the ruthlessness, the determination, the nerveless fearlessness to challenge one after another the most desperate of Chicago's criminals and best them at their own game?

It is this secret that will be bared for the first time in the pages to follow.

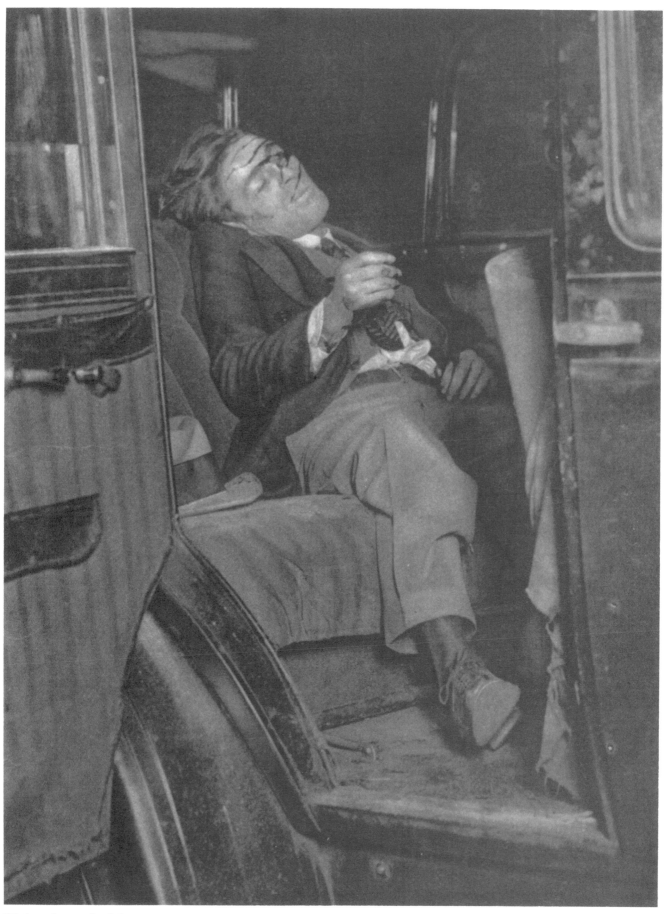

"Taken for a ride" is gangland's own phrase for what it does to those who break its laws. Here is Thomas Ulo's body, found riddled with bullets in a stolen car in Brooklyn. Only the manner of his death proclaims him a victim of gangs for he was not listed as a racketeer.

Chicago tried to keep Capone out of the town after he got a criminal record in Philadelphia. Police watched his home for days but he showed up at the detective bureau and asked what they had on him. The answer was; "Nothing!" And so he stepped outside and had his picture taken with the detective chiefs.

CHAPTER THREE: How Al's Execution Squad Works

BEFORE WE plunge into the history of Al Capone's spectacular and bloody rise, let us consider a few of the achievements that brought him to the top of the pile.

Just as any great leader has his high spots, so has Al. Washington had his Valley Forge, and Pershing had his St. Mihiel.

Al has yet to meet his Waterloo—but wait.

Let us look first at the way society rids itself of its enemies. There's the long, cumbersome trial, the appeals to higher courts, reprieves, months of delay and then—maybe the convicted man gets a stiff jolt but escapes the death penalty.

That sort of stuff wouldn't go with Al.

How could gangdom survive to beat the law and prove stronger than the forces of government if gangdom didn't have more effective methods of operating?

When Al first started, of course, he wasn't so hot at the business. A man can't be too particular when he's beginning. But let's consider some of the outstanding jobs that have been credited to Al's fine Italian hand.

There's a genial little chap named Dion O'Banion who has been making a nuisance of himself for all his smiling ways. Something has to happen to Dion. He has ambitions to rule too much territory. He's cutting in on Al's profits. So Dion goes on the spot.

Don't think that's as simple as it sounds. It takes a man with brains to engineer it properly, and Al has 'em.

First, let's get the lay. Dion spends much of his time in his flower shop, where he puts up a legitimate front as a business man. Step by step the execution of O'Banion is worked out according to the lay of the land, his personal habits, and his protective means.

Dion's to be put on the spot in his own flower shop. That's the place for him.

He carries three guns, and does away with a bodyguard. How to bump him off without injury to the execution squad, then, is the next problem. The brains of the homicide squad spends some time on this matter. And finally a clever plan is evolved, one that should work like a charm.

Doubtless the men named for the job were carefully rehearsed as to each part they would play. Al's executions always have something of the theatrical about them—rising to a dramatic climax that literally knocks the audience out of its seats.

Thus the stage was set. The curtain rises.

"Hello, Deanie? Say, we're sending after some flowers for Mike Merlo's funeral."

The speaker heard O'Banion reply that he would be glad to be of service in the matter. And O'Banion was therefore on hand for the spotlight.

Mike Merlo, dead chief of the Sicilian Union, was to be buried in style. Thousands of dollars worth of flowers must be bought, and O'Banion could, as usual, make good use of the money. He expected, then, some visitors on a friendly mission.

The three men assigned to this job drove up in a car, following the cue of the 'phone call. They entered the shop, and Dion came out of the rear room to greet them. The crucial moment is arriving. All three killers must act their part—there must be no false move or expression to give them away.

Smiles masked the killers' eyes. O'Banion thrust

"He loved flowers and he loved killing" was said of Dion O'Banion before he was put on the spot in the first "glad hand kill" in Chicago's gang war.

Crash! One—two—three—four—five blasting shots tore into him as he shivered and swayed on his feet, held before the spitting gun by both hands.

Then they let go of him. He fell to the floor, and the gun was pressed to his head. A sixth shot roared in the flower shop.

Unhurriedly, the three men made their exit, and stepped into the waiting car.

The play was over. It was curtains for Dion O'Banion.

Don't you applaud the little drama? Then you don't appreciate the fine art of murder. What—no curtain calls for the author of it?

Of course there are—from O'Banion's horrified friends and allies. They wanted to lay hands on the author of this little play, and they wanted him very much. Immediately the word went forth that Capone and his partner Torrio would pay for the killing of O'Banion.

NOW THAT we have seen Capone's drama, let's find out how his enemies work. And here we put the finger on the very reason for Al's tremendous power. He is putting a sixteen cylinder brain against the efforts of a bunch of four cylinder affairs—with three cylinders missing out of the four. They just haven't got the brain power to buck against the man who rules Chicago today.

Hymie Weiss, daring, clever in his way, took up the vengeance trail and made his headquarters in O'Banion's flower shop. He wasn't afraid of Capone, or Torrio either. He'd get 'em, and get 'em quick! Thus spoke Hymie, and hopefully the enemies of Capone rallied round him.

So Hymie gritted his teeth and with his comrades and a flock of machine guns drove hellbent for Cicero, to rub out Capone. If I remember rightly, there were twelve cars in that mad army of invasion that roared into Cicero.

As soon as they reached the town bullets began to fly from their machine guns. Al Capone, they must have thought, would be standing in the middle of the street waiting to be killed.

Bullets poured into Al's cafe at the Hawthorne Hotel, headquarters of his gang. Windows crashed, splinters flew. But no lead found the soft plump body of The Big Shot.

Now do you wonder what Al survives? It will take a much cleverer man than he to rub out Capone.

So there was Hymie, gnawing his fingernails over his failure and wishing he was bright enough to write a little play like the one in which O'Banion figured.

He still made use of the headquarters in O'Banion's flower shop building. He still went to and fro along the sidewalk path where O'Banion's killers had stepped into their getaway car.

How did the master killer go about it to snuff out the life of this impudent enemy who had issued

On these two pages you'll find reasons why Al Capone reigns supreme. Hymie Weiss (above) almost became a big shot when he succeeded O'Banion as chief of the North Siders, but Hymie didn't know how to kill. His blundering cost him his life, and proved to Al how swell machine guns work.

out his hand to meet the one extended by the man in the middle of the visiting delegation. In Dion's left hand he held a pair of scissors with which he had been trimming flowers.

Suddenly O'Banion read the expression on the killer's stern face.

With Dion's right hand gripped firmly by the center man, he could not wrest it free. He dropped the scissors, but the man at his left seized his wrist.

Helpless, O'Banion saw the deadly weapon of execution appear. Before he could cry out the first slug ripped into his body.

MURDER BY WHOLESALE STAGED WITH THE PRECISION OF A MASTER DRAMATIST

The Valentine's Day massacre proved to Chicago gangsters that Al was their Master, for in this wholesale slaughter of Bugs Moran's army, the cleverest stunt in gang history was accomplished and Al was freed of of his most powerful enemy.

All Chicago gasped at the ruthless murder of Bugs Moran's hardboiled gang, but when the bodies were hauled away Al Capone was left in peace, and Bugs ducked for Minnesota to hide for his life. Two of the slayers who left death behind them in the garage on St. Valentine's Day, wore the uniforms of policemen. The evidence is that whoever planned this astounding crime intended to "put on the spot" at least ten members of the gang which was then challenging Capone's supremacy. Three of the men, including Moran, escaped by good fortune and have thus far dodged gang death.

A general without an army was Bugs Moran, shown here with his wife, after seven of his men were lined up and filled with hot lead.

a bold-faced challenge in the Cicero bombardment?

He was as patient as Fate itself. First there was a reconnoitre of the premises, though they were already well known to all. There was the door to the flower shop. There was the stair door beside it. There was the Holy Name church across the way, where Dion O'Banion had once served as acolyte. There was the rear entrance that let onto an areaway and a side street.

Does the master killer cling to the technique he used here once before? He does not. He knows that Hymie Weiss would never thrust out a hand to the middle man of three who approached him with friendly smiles.

He must arrange a new plan. And so it comes about that a young man took a room at 740 North State Street, next door to Weiss' headquarters. Its windows commanded an angling view of the sidewalk in front of the shop. At about the same time a woman took rooms at No. 1 West Superior Street which commanded a view of the shop's rear door.

One after the other, three men sifted into each of these rooms. One by one three or more violin cases were opened and three machine guns were set up at the windows of these two rooms.

And then began a death watch. Nobody knows or perhaps ever will know the number of times little Hymie Weiss passed before the muzzles of those machine guns before they let go. There was no hurry.

One by one the three men who sat at each window lighted, smoked and tossed aside their cigarets. One

day passed. Two days passed. Death held its hand over Hymie Weiss and waited till the time should be auspicious.

WHO COMMANDED these six men? Who told them when it was time to shoot or when it was necessary to hold back the murderous fire because the street was too crowded, because someone was with Weiss who must not be harmed? Who had issued the command that placed the men there in the first place and whose mind had conceived the machine gun nest of gangdom?

The master killer had given these orders, laid these plans. His handiwork proclaims him.

And then came the moment when the three men in the flat on State Street tossed aside their cigarets and leaned forward.

Hymie Weiss, who had led the demonstration against the killing of O'Banion, stepped down from a motor car. As he did so, the Tommy guns let go in the upper room next door to his own headquarters.

Tac tac tac! Leaden hail was flying in the street.

Little Hymie fell with ten bullets in his body. Patrick Murray, one of his beer peddlers, fell beside him with seven bullet wounds. W. W. O'Brien, a criminal lawyer, Benjamin Jacobs, a politician, and Sam Peller, Weiss' chauffeur, were mowed down but lived.

So sure had been the plans for Weiss' death that two men died where one had been marked. Three others were saved at the hospital.

Six of the Valentine Massacre victims: Adam Heyer, John May and Al Weinshank—

The plan was air tight. The witness did not see the killers. When the police arrived the upper room held nothing but three chairs and a pile of cigaret stubs. The ambush at the rear door was not even discovered till several days later, after it, too, was vacant.

But even this was not the ultimate development of execution in the mind of the master criminal. It was to be used later against Joseph Aiello and just as effectively. It was to be tried by others against Capone and Lombardo but without even a chance of success.

There came a time when the Capone supremacy was to be threatened once more, when Aiello and Bugs Moran were to execute successful coups against the king, when they were to make the unsuccessful attempts on his life that roused the Big Fellow once more to a supreme effort.

AND THEN was murder demonstrated in its ultimate form. And this time the exquisite planning and execution of the master mind were again in evidence.

Once more long preparation is indicated. The

—and Frank Clark, Frank Guzenberg, and Pete Guzenberg. So t o u g h was Frank Guzenberg that he lived long enough to get to a hospital.

Seven of the deadliest guns on the north side, and all killed without firing a shot in return! How this was accomplished sounds like a movie plot, but it happened in real life, as this picture proves.

project apparently was nothing less than the complete extermination of one entire group of the enemy.

Bugs Moran and his mob that hung out in Heyer's garage, the S. M. C. Cartage Company, 2122 North Clark Street, had been involved in the death of Pasqualino Lolordo, Capone successor to Tony Lombardo as head of the Unione Sicilione.

The master killer began an intensive study of the habits of this gang. He found that the men frequently congregated in the garage. Here was the opportunity that might be developed, but nothing was left to chance.

Someone, inspired by this master killer, began doing a modest business in hijacked liquor with the Moran gang. A telephone call, a deal, the delivery of a truck load of booze, the pay-off and confidence was developed. How many truckloads were delivered in this way may never be known, but there

came another telephone call on February 13, 1929.

"O. K. Bring it around tomorrow morning about 10:30. The boys will be there to get their cut."

Moran apparently suspected nothing, but chance made him late for the rendezvous and also delayed Willie Marks and Ted Newberry. But the Gusenbergs, Frank and Pete were on hand. So was John May, the safe-blower. So was Al Weinshank, the speakeasy proprietor. James Clark, bank robber suspect, and Adam Heyer, owner of the garage sat with them in the big storage room where seven trucks waited for a quick rush to Detroit that afternoon with a big rum-running coup in prospect.

There also was a young optometrist, a Dr. Schwimmer, who had been playing around with the mob, dropping in for a chat with the notorious ones for the thrill he got out of this association.

They all come to the same end—usually a shot from the back. Here lies William Simpson, dockside gangster whose outfit worked New York and Chicago. Detective Hammel is examining the death gun. The dock racket is simply that of dominating by ruthlessness the stevedores or dock wallopers on the water front, driving from the job those who will not pay tribute to the bully who thus establishes himself. A percentage of the daily wage of each man is collected if he is to hold his job.

The time for the coup arrived. Moran and two of his men were late to the rendezvous. This could not be allowed to hold up the proceedings. At 10:30, or a little after, the pseudo squad car drew up a door or two from Heyer's garage. Five men got out and entered the building.

The men garbed in the blue uniforms of the police, went directly into the garage where Moran's men waited. The other two, bearing newspaper covered packages, stood in the passageway that led to the big room.

The killer's men knew the psychology of the Moran gang. They knew that there would be no resistance to a police raid. They knew it would be merely an incident in the gangsters' lives, that they would submit with smiles on their lips, knowing that the fix would be in before the squad car reached the police station.

The key to the whole scene must be the impersonation of the policemen. There must be no slip here, no misjudging of the gang's secret thoughts.

Against the brick wall of the garage stood the seven doomed men, arms raised, waiting for the coppers to get the wagon and be done with the farce. Probably the hardboiled Guzenberg brothers winked at each other as they stood there, grinning because a few dumb coppers thought they could send a gangster to jail and make it stick.

The master criminal expected this reaction. No reason why a gangster should pull a rod on a copper and get into a lot of unnecessary fuss with the law. The Moran boys would figure on having the gang's "mouthpieces" on hand with bail if it came to that.

Abruptly one of the coppers gave a low call.

"All right, boys!"

Two men stepped quickly in from the garage doorway. In their hands were Thompson sub-machine guns!

They were in position before the men, faces to the wall, knew what was up.

The brick garage echoed suddenly to the crash of those deadly guns. Red flashes spat death as the lead rattled from the machine guns, and sprayed back and forth across the line of men. First across the heads, then lower, as the screaming victims collapsed.

Quickly the executioners inspected the bodies. Two still lived. Sawed-off shotguns blew out their brains.

Then the executioners wheeled. The two men who had carried the machine guns gave up their guns to the coppers. They held their hands high in the air.

And from the garage in which the machine guns had roared to attract spectators outside the building came the first getaway parade in the history of murder. Those who looked out curiously after the rat-a-ta-tat of the shooting saw three policemen apparently arresting two men in plain clothes who walked slowly with their hands in the air to the black squad car and then were driven away.

But the task had not yet been completed. Seven men lay dead or dying in the fatal garage on that St. Valentine's morning but there were still three full uniforms of the police to be destroyed or sent back to the place from which they had come. There was still the big black Cadillac to be cut up with oxy-acetelene torches and disposed of where only by chance were the pieces recognized and then without harm to the killers.

Here was murder dramatized and staged in the perfect production.

O'Banion's pal, Three-gun Louie Alterie, used to be a cowboy before he enlisted in the gang war. Chicago got too hot and he went back west.

But Bugs Moran and his two satellites had been late to their own execution. The story goes that they saw the squad car, were deceived into thinking a raid was in progress and drove on around the block without halting to look in. The production had been too complete, too perfect, if any fault at all were to be found in it.

This is gang murder raised to one of the arts. This is execution under efficiency engineers. This is the handiwork of the master mind of murder somewhere in the Capone organization for, as Bugs Moran blurted out before he thought when he heard the truth:

"Only Capone kills like that."

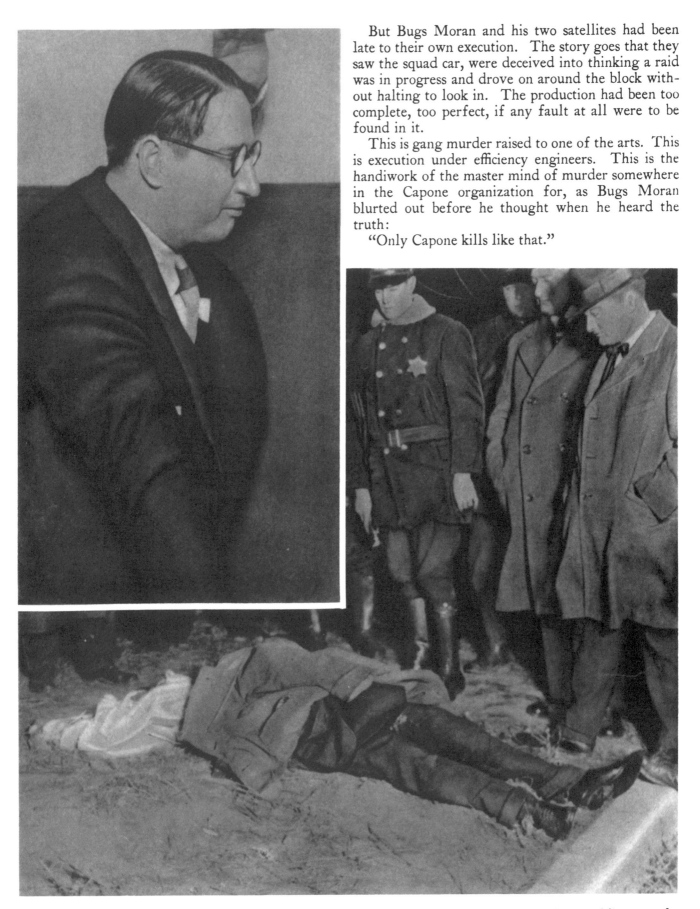

William McSwiggin (above, alive; below, dead) who died under gang guns, as shown above, while a member of the prosecutor's staff of Cook county, was one of the first attorneys in Chicago to defend Capone when he got into a jam. He was in the company of two gangsters when he was killed. One of them was a man he had just prosecuted successfully. Did McSwiggin step into the path of gang bullets aimed at his companion or was he the intended victim?

You'd never think this smiling lad bore the tough name of Scarface Al. But at that it looks as though he had merely smiled for the photographer. Al dresses well, you'll notice, but there's nothing very flashy about this get-up or any of the others he wears on the street.

"Taking 'em for a ride" is too much trouble in New York. Here they took Teddy Pandola for a walk, and the results were the same anyway. Note the cameraman setting up his box to shoot the closeup shown in the circle.

CHAPTER FOUR: Capone's History Writ in Blood

NOW, AFTER convincing you—I hope—that Al Capone is all that one could expect in a Master Criminal, let us consider something of his history. You've seen how he works, and what sort of a man he is. How did he get that way?

That's the story I want to spin for you now.

A threat of death brought Al Capone to the scene of his future grandeur. The threat was directed at Big Jim Colosimo, proprietor of a famous cafe bearing his name at 2126 S. Wabash Avenue.

Colosimo was the founder of the Chicago underworld dynasty. He came up from the gutter as literally as any man ever did in this world, for he got his start as a street sweeper.

An Italian immigrant of the nineties, he had been water boy for a section gang when he took his first step on the political ladder by accepting the lowly position of a white wing in the First Ward.

In this capacity he became popular with his fellow white wings and presently attracted the notice of Michael Hinky Dink Kenna and Bathhouse John Coughlin, the alderman of the ward. These two were a pair of rare birds. At the Workingmen's Exchange in those days Kenna sold the largest schooner of beer ever offered for five cents within the memory of man. Bathhouse John, his opposite in almost every characteristic, was addicted to fancy vests and what passed among his proteges for poetry.

They found in the youthful and black-eyed Colosimo the makings of a political power and cultivated him to the point where he organized his fellow white wings into a social and athletic club which he voted as a unit when election day rolled around.

In recognition of this yeoman service Hinky Dink and Bathhouse John conferred upon Colosimo the coveted order of precinct captaincy which carried with it certain appurtenances in the old levee district bisected by Twenty-second Street.

From this position the natural steps were to those of pool room proprietor, saloon keeper, dive keeper and eventually proprietor of Colosimo's Cafe.

Big Jim blossomed out then into a ward boss who dressed the part and looked it. He had money, he had influence, he had diamonds enough on his person to match the electric lights of his cafe sign.

But the eminence of Big Jim brought him worries of a sort not unusual to those of his kind who walk in the ways of prosperity. One day when the gray-clad postman had left the morning's mail at the cafe, Big Jim held a letter in his hand and gazed thoughtfully out toward the street door.

He had received the Italian acolade, a letter from the Mafia. This and letters following brought him assurance at least that he was one of the big shots. He had been singled out for threats of kidnapping and ransom. Later letters promised torture and death. The remedy for all this would be a sum of money to be contributed to an emissary of the Mafia in ways and by means further to be elucidated.

COLOSIMO might have paid the money and given the matter no further thought and if he had it is interesting to speculate what might have become of two certain persons of later importance to the Colosimo dynasty.

But he didn't. He knew, being wise to his day, his race and generation, that whatever sum he might disgorge would be only a first installment.

Big Jim, sitting with the letters in his hand, determined not to go to the police, not to go to the political overlords whom he served, not to do any of the ordinary things that might be expected of him, but to go to New York and bring himself back what has

Here's the bird who was wary of the photographer. He is Johnny Torrio who brought Al to Chicago.

come to be termed in the language of his empire a "gun."

What occult influences guided him in his choice may never be known but it is a matter of historic fact that he went with unerring instinct to the bailiwick of the Five Points gang which had produced such notorious characters as Lefty Louie and Gyp the Blood and brought back with him an inoffensive looking "gun" my the name of Torrio.

Torrio was 29 and came west to grow up with the country. Shortly after his arrival in Chicago, Colosimo received a visit in person from his correspondents whose billets doux he had failed to answer.

Three men came into the cafe and informed him that he had only one day more of life to live unless he produced $25,000. Colosimo turned the matter over to Torrio who advised Colosimo to meet the men with the money the following afternoon at the Archer Avenue viaduct.

If Colosimo was disappointed in his strong arm man, he gave no sign. The visitors departed and rallied around the viaduct at the appointed time. Colosimo did not appear, but four men with sawed-off shotguns converged upon the three at the appointed time and paid them off in messengers of death.

Thereafter, Colosimo's anonymous correspondence fell off.

YEARS CAME and went. Torrio had grown up with the country and had surrounded Chicago with a wreath of dives. Big Jim continued to operate in the vicinity of Twenty-second Street but his chief of staff was branching out.

The World War had come and gone. Prohibition had arrived in the constitutional sense at least. Chicago was a welter of bootleggers. Gin gold lurked wherever man had elbow room to tip a glass.

Then brazen opportunity burst down the door at Colosimo's, took him and Torrio to the rooftops and

Here is Big Jim Colosimo dead in spite of the fact that he had Johnny Torrio and Al Capone for bodyguard. Both the boys were questioned about his death and they succeeded to the throne he set up in the dynasty of Chicago's underworld.

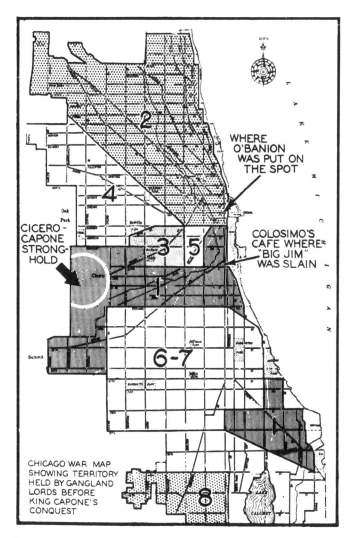

Major principalities as they appeared before the completion of King Capone's conquest are graphically shown on this war map of Chicago. (1) Capone territory; (2) North Side gang; (3) the Druggans; (4) "Klondike" O'Donnell, (5) The Gennas, Capone allies; (6-7) "Spike" O'Donnell, Joe Saltis and the Sheldon gang; (8) Joe Juliano. Map in next column shows how he conquered them all.

The other was Alphonse Capone.

Cosmano was too tough for Yale's bullets, though he languished for a time in the hospital.

Capone remained after Yale had returned to New York.

Capone was the good man Torrio had named for the job.

Thus came Capone to Chicago, land of bilk and money, to carve for himself a generous fortune with a butcher knife that had no regard for other fellows' skins.

Thus began the maneuver of the fates that made a gangster the most influential man in Chicago and was to leave the entire city with its vast ramifications of business and industry paying tribute to him.

Thus began the career in Chicago of the man who declares today that they won't let him go into a legitimate business.

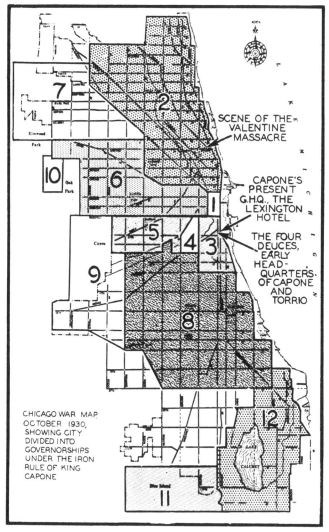

Map showing divisions of the Chicago monarchy with governors representing the King: (1) Jake Gusick, (2) Ted Newberry, (3) Joe Gusick, (4) Jack McGurn, (5) George Druggan, Capone ally; (6) "Klondike" O'Donnell, Capone ally; (7) Claude Maddox, (8) "Spike" O'Donnell and the Sheldon gang, with Danny Stanton in charge for the King; (9) Ralph Capone, (10) Joe Montana, (11) the old Juliano gang, (12) Joe Genaro.

showed them a promised land of fabulous wealth.

But the telephone bell was ringing in Colosimo's office. A friend of his had called him up to talk with him.

"This is Little Jimmy," the voice said. "I jus' wan' to let you know I am gon' keel you."

The telephone clicked. "Little Jimmy" Cosmano had not remained on the line to discuss with his intended victim the time and method of death.

Colosimo knew when to take a joke but this he knew was no joke. He called in Torrio and asked if he didn't want to get a good man to help him with his duties as muscle man.

Torrio did, and named the man. Big Jim went back to the Five Points gang in New York and brought home with him not one, but two "good" men.

One was Frankie Yale, born Francesco Uale, who took care of the Little Jimmy Cosmano matter.

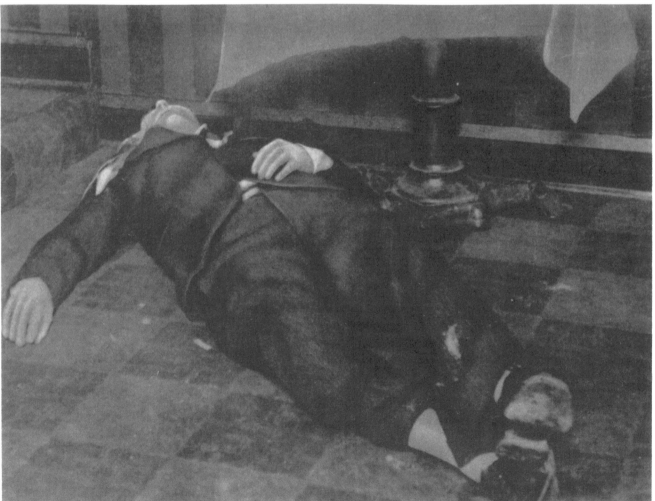

William "Gunner" McPadden (above) and Hugh "Stubby" McGovern (below) carried heavy guns for Danny Stanton, a Capone henchman, but George Maloney of "Bubs" Quinlan's gang got them both at a New Year celebration and was acquitted when witnesses failed to identify him as the killer.

CHAPTER FIVE: Capone In On "The Fix"

OLD MAN DEATH, having played the card that brought Capone to Chicago, now set events moving rapidly for that young man.

He was a diamond in the rough, this Capone. Twenty-three years old, he had lived the life of a gamin since he left school in the fourth grade. But for the machinations of his guardian angel, Death, he might have gone on from minor pillaging to the major activity of looting warehouses on the New York wharves.

His patron saint had left his calling card twice, however, before he left New York, for Capone had been questioned in two murder cases involving the Five Point gang.

When he came to Johnny Torrio and Colosimo in Chicago he was lacking in the social graces; a hard lad with a quick temper and lightning with fists or gun. That was early in 1920. He was not then the dapper figure of a man he is today, though the Neapolitan chubbiness had not yet developed.

But he had a head that even then could be used for other purposes than growing a patent-leather pompadour. His first move was to establish a front for himself—some innocent business shop as headquarters.

Torrio's headquarters were on the ground floor of 2222 South Wabash Avenue, named from its number the Four Deuces. The four-story brick building housed a saloon and cafe, a gambling house and a floor or two occupied by more or less lovely ladies.

In one corner of this building, Capone opened a shop. His cards read, "Alphonse Capone, Second-Hand Furniture Dealer, 2220 South Wabash Avenue." Inside the shop there was, indeed, second-hand furniture. The stage was properly set. Capone needed no further props.

Big Jim Colosimo, though he had built up the machine for which he was famous, didn't know how to handle it on a fast track. He fell in love with one of the entertainers in his cafe, blossomed out with new decorations in the place and handsome clothes for himself and left the rough work to his right and left hand, Torrio and Capone. By and by Big Jim was just a nuisance to his lieutenants; a pimple on the proboscis of progress.

Jim divorced his wife and married the lady, Miss Dale Winter, a musical comedy singer, and went la de dah for a few days. Then he turned up dead—murdered in the hall of his cafe by an assistant who hid in the checkroom.

Torrio and Capone were questioned about the little matter but nothing came of it except an elaborate funeral for Big Jim and reorganization of the gang business by Messrs. Torrio and Capone.

"Klondike" O'Donnell led one of the O'Donnell gangs in the early days of the beer war on the West Side. "Klondike" is Al's friend—don't confuse him with "Spike" O'Donnell.

THIS WAS in 1920 and the Capone publicity department opened up two years later. Capone, it seems, had been cut in by Torrio on the Chicago rackets and the boys were ready to branch out and meet competition.

The first news story to be published about the future king of gangland and Emperor of the Underworld, didn't make first page.

It seems that Mr. Capone, in the course of an evening's relaxation, grew hilarious and, in company with three men and a woman drove riotously down North Wabash Avenue and crashed his automobile into a taxicab at East Randolph Street.

The taxicab was parked at the curb and in it was Fred Krause, the driver. Capone's companions fled. Capone got out of the automobile, drew a revolver,

While the nation seethed with news of the Valentine Day Massacre, Al Capone at Miami beach, was being photographed with Bill Cunningham, former All-American football player, and Jack Sharkey, pugilist. They were snapped at a beach resort.

displayed a deputy sheriff's badge and threatened to shoot Krause.

A street-car motorman jumped from his car and advised Capone to put up the weapon, but was in turn threatened with a speedy release from life, according to contemporary accounts.

Policemen came. Capone was arrested. Krause was taken away in an ambulance. And the one newspaper that printed the story announced that "Caponi," as it spelled the name, would appear in South Clark Street court the next day.

Capone didn't appear. The case didn't come to trial although Al faced three charges; assault with an automobile, driving while intoxicated, and carrying concealed weapons. The fix was in.

Mr. Alphonse Capone, second-hand furniture dealer, it appears, was a special deputy sheriff. He was in right with the political powers. Remnants of Big Jim Colosimo's influence, or the rising power of Johnny Torrio, or perhaps, the prestige of Capone himself, had sufficed to fix the police, the courts and the prosecutor's office.

CHAPTER SIX: Did Al Bump Off Joe Howard?

THERE HAS been talk of digging up the Joe Howard case against Capone. There has been heard the boast that the Howard killing would be used to send Capone to the chair.

But Capone still vacations in his $375,000 home on Palm Island near Miami Beach and Capone, with 14 bodyguards, still roams as free as the breezes.

Who was Joe Howard and where does he fit into the picture?

Back in 1924 when Johnny Torrio and Al Capone operated the Four Deuces at 2222 South Wabash Avenue, that notorious dive, den and brothel was the hangout for men who were to become world famous for their lives and deaths in Chicago gangdom.

But Joe Howard didn't rate a membership in this ultra exclusive club. Joe was a big joke to most of these illustrious gangsters. He was just a bum.

In an earlier day he might have been regarded as a hard egg but in Chicago's beerage he was only a fairly successful burglar and safe-blower and he had no more than three notches on his old gun. No, Joe didn't rate in the nobility.

Joe didn't hang around the Four Deuces. Half a block away was a saloon called Heinie's Place where the second rate guns foregathered and here Joe loafed and drank and talked about himself.

In Joe's estimation he was a tough baby and he made conversation about it. But something had to be done to prove his point. It was in the days when hijacking was the new thing and booze running was getting organized.

You had to be tough to be a hijacker and Joe had his own authority for the belief that this was up his street. He chose to back his words by deeds and tried to rob a distillery warehouse in North Clark Street.

Somehow a policeman happened along, caught him in the act and hauled him in.

But Joe had his share of influence among the lesser politicians. His case dragged along for months and was dismissed.

Joe next turned his attention to hijacking and this time luck was with him. He took two trucks in one night and could not forbear to boast about it over a glass or two in Heinie's place.

Chicago murder methods originated in New York, from where they were imported by Al Capone. Here is Geraldo Hedmano, the victim of underworld vengeance at the wheel of his taxicab. Somebody drove alongside and bumped him off.

NOTHING happened that night.

But the next evening when Joe was sitting behind the cigar counter in Heinie's place about six o'clock, basking in the limelight of his exploit and indulging his love of boasting, the door opened and two men came in.

George Bilton and David Runelsbeck who roomed in the neighborhood told the story to the police afterward. Bilton was an automobile mechanic and Runelsbeck a carpenter. They had stopped in for a drink on their way home.

The men came in and walked up to Joe, according to Runelsbeck. Joe stood up.

"Hello, Al," he said and thrust out his hand in friendly greeting. On his face was a smile. Here he must have thought was the final acolade. The Big Shots were taking notice of him at last.

But the man toward whom he had put out his friendly hand had a revolver in his and he fired six shots into the bum who aspired to be a tough baby.

Capone was ordered arrested for the crime on bulletins that went to all stations within thirty minutes. Michael Hughes, chief of detectives, after he had talked with the elderly carpenter, announced that Capone had killed Joe Howard and described how it was done.

Here it was 1924 and still the Chicago papers couldn't get Capone's name right. A morning newspaper printed his picture as "Tony (Scarface) Capone, also known as Al Brown, who killed Joe Howard in Heinie Jacob's saloon."

It was May 8 with the first breath of real spring in the air. Perhaps that is why Heinie Jacobs couldn't remember what had happened the next day. Maybe it was the shock of witnessing the crime that made Runelsbeck deny he could recognize the killer the next day. Something must have happened to make George Bilton disappear from his old haunts.

CAPONE was nowhere to be found. A month later he walked into a police station and said:

"I hear the police are looking for me. What for?"

When Joe Howard's death was mentioned he declared he had been out of town that day, that he was a second-hand furniture dealer and didn't know Torrio or anything about the Four Deuces.

"Talk to my lawyer," he said.

William H. McSwiggin, assistant state attorney, who was to die in a machine gun barrage within two years, declared he had the case dead to rights. The coroner's investigation was ended in July with the verdict that Joe Howard died of bullets fired by one or more unknown, white male persons.

Al Capone was not further molested about the untimely taking off of Mr. Howard. If the matter is again brought up with any intent to send Mr. Capone to the hot seat, there will be a long, hard fight if any witnesses remain who can be consulted on the subject.

Veteran of the early beer wars, "Spike" O'Donnell is here seen on trial as member of a slot machine ring recently brought to trial in Chicago. One of Al's few surviving enemies.

The theory seems to be that in these days Al Capone was doing his own torpedo work just as many a young struggler in the business world is forced to attend to the menial tasks of his enterprise before he is able to put on a sufficient force to attend to these drudgeries.

He was questioned once about the deaths of Jerry O'Connor, Spot Bucher and Georgie Meeghan. But nothing ever came of that.

The South Side Gang of which these three were adherents had determined to argue with Capone and Torrio about the liquor rights in what is known as the Kerry Patch. It had its beer drummers, among whom were O'Connor, Bucher and Meeghan.

THE METHODS of these three and of others at the same time was to go into a saloon or speakeasy and demand:

"Who you buying from?"

O'Connor and his partners gave them twenty-four hours to decide they were buying from O'Donnell of the South Side Gang. If that wasn't enough they administered a beating with fists and clubbed revolvers. If that didn't do, more was forthcoming.

One night they made five calls, administered five beatings, and retired to 5358 South Lincoln Street to meet the boss, Spike O'Donnell, and have a little lunch following a hard night's work.

Suddenly four men burst in upon them. Daniel McFall, a deputy sheriff, ordered "Hands up" and the South Siders scattered.

Just then a short, stocky man, wearing a gray raincoat and carrying a sawed-off shotgun appeared. McFall signaled and he backed out. The South Siders were then chased into the street where shotgun and revolver shots resounded and Jerry O'Connor died with a bullet through his heart.

Meeghan and Bucher had ten days more to live. On September 17 their car halted at Laflin Street and Garfield Boulevard to obey a traffic signal and revolver bullets and shotgun slugs mowed them down from a green touring car that had pulled alongside.

Then followed hullaballoo.

Capone, among those questioned, reiterated that he was a second-hand furniture dealer and was not identified by any South Siders. Torrio disappeared. McFall was indicted and acquitted. There was a police shakeup.

After he had lost a brother and some other gunmen imported for his cause, Spike O'Donnell burst out at a detective bureau session declaring:

"I can whip this bird Capone with bare fists any time he wants to step out in the open and fight like a man."

But just what that had to do with the beer killings was never fully explained. Finally O'Donnell retired and Capone-Torrio beer was served in Kerry Patch.

Torrio toured Europe and bought his peasant mother an estate and an automobile with a chauffeur in Italy.

Capone boosted salaries of his torpedoes to $25,000 a week.

"Professional bad man of Chicago's Little Italy" was the unofficial title of Philip Gnolfo but even the bad man has no chance when gangsters go gunning. They drove alongside his car, forced it to the curb and cut loose with machine-gun fire. Two companions of Gnolfo were wounded together with an innocent boy of fifteen who happened to be passing the scene of vengeance.

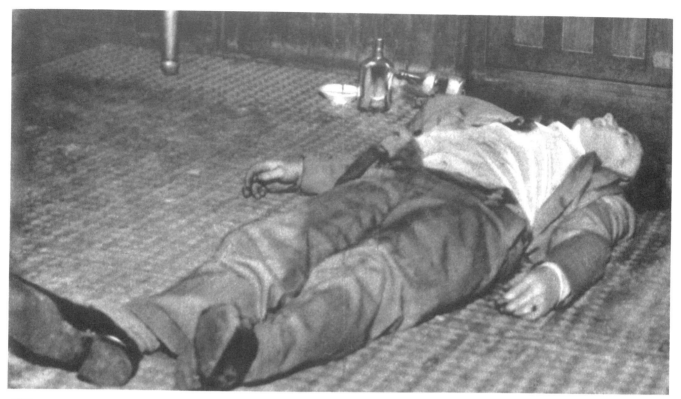

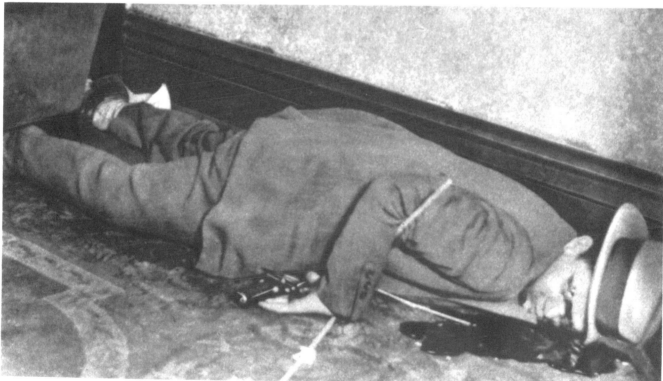

Two of Chicago's bombing extortionists will play their g a m e no more. They were trapped in the apartment of Jack Hayes, an i n t e n d e d victim. Four policemen were hidden in the flat when they arrived. Hayes was ill. In the gun battle that followed, Joe Altmeier, one of the police officers, was mortally wounded, but "Limpy" White (top) and John Vitaco (below) were shot to death. Vitaco died with his automatic clutched in his hand. Hayes, the intended victim, was slain as he lay ill in bed in the midst of the gun battle. The dead men were m e m b e r s of Chicago's notorious pineapple terrorist crew who for months kept the city in fear of their depredations. They tried the bombing shakedown on innocent business men who were notified that if they did not contribute they would find their business places in ruins. Hundreds are said to have paid for immunity which could never be bought since the game, worked once, was easier a second time.

The eastern front of gangland is coming to be as bloody as Chicago. The body of James Tinerello (above), gangster and convict, was taken from a snowdrift where it had been hidden by murderers. Thomas Duffy (below) was found shot to death in "dead man's lot" on Long Island.

CHAPTER SEVEN: The Capture of Cicero

THE CAPTURE of a city may sometimes be termed the birth of an empire.

Al Capone captured a city and ruled it with an iron hand.

The place was Cicero, a suburb of Chicago. Things had got too hot downtown. A former soda jerker had got ambitious in the suburban town.

This soda jerker had accomplished from his humble position in Cicero, what Big Jim Colosimo had done with his humbler one in the earlier day of Chicago. He had won friends over the soda counter. He had grown to be precinct captain, then to be ward boss and Governor Small had finally named him Republican committeeman from Cicero.

His name was Ed Konvalinka. He had an idea. He mentioned it to Edward Vogel who passed it on to Louis La Cava, a Capone man.

Presently the soda jerker and Scarface Capone met and agreed. They selected a political ticket for Cicero. Konvalinka declared that if Capone could elect it on April 1, he could have his own way in Cicero.

Election day arrived in the suburban city of 70,000. It was probably the strangest election day in the history of any American city. Sluggings and kidnappings. Gangster cars racing through the streets. Citizens terrorized. Policemen chased from their beats with gun shots. The right guys turned out to vote while Al Capone's brother, Frank, was being killed in one of the many battles.

When it was all over, the Konvalinka ticket was in power. Konvalinka, the Republican committeeman, made good his promise.

One hundred sixty-one bars ran wide open in Cicero after that. Handbooks, gambling dens, dog tracks and the like did the biggest business in modern history. Five hundred harlots flocked to Stickney, the adjoining commonwealth under Johnny Torrio's tutelage.

Within four months the Capone-Torrio take was $200,000 a week.

Eddie Tancl fought while the rest of Cicero took it lying down. Tancl was a saloonkeeper. He wouldn't buy Capone beer. He wouldn't pay tribute. He fought and died with Leo Kilmas, his waiter, when Myles O'Donnell and James J. Doherty brought the enforcers' instruments and shot it out with him. Then Capone and Torrio did business at the Tancl stand.

O'Donnell and Doherty, prosecuted by William McSwiggin, were acquitted.

And thus Al Capone waxed famous by providing for his boys, keeping the territory free of interlopers, and ruling with an iron hand. But Cicero wasn't big enough to hold a lad like Al.

He looked about him for new worlds to conquer and the new world lay at his door—the city of Chicago. What he had done in the little suburb he was ambitious to do in the greater city. He laid his plans carefully. He gave notice that nothing was to stand in his way. He permitted other gangsters to join his forces and played square with them until they tried to double-cross him.

But when, for any reason, there came a break between him and his men, the guns came shooting and death was the umpire of the controversy.

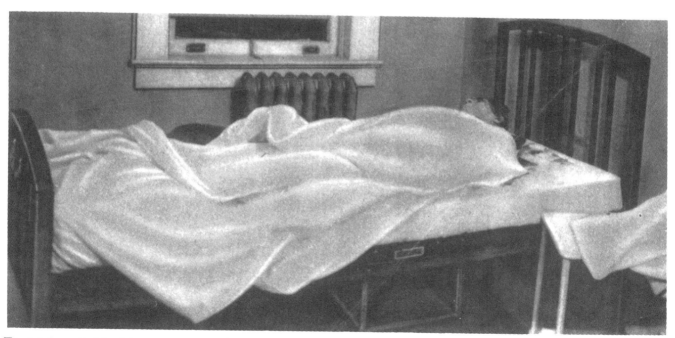

Even a hospital bed is no sanctuary in gangland. Here is one of the Newark grape racketeers, John Pacelli, called The Ape, shot to death in a New Jersey hospital.

Dion O'Banion was proprietor of this flower shop where he was shot to death in the "glad hand" murder. The picture shows the crowd that gathered about after the killers had made their getaway in a car.

CHAPTER EIGHT: O'Banion Declares War

DION O'BANION was in those days an ally of Capone and Torrio. They were called the Big Three. O'Banion has been termed the most powerful of the triumvirate. But Death sided with the other two men when they fell out with the Irish "Deaney."

Torrio had engineered the alliance with the little florist who always delivered his district at election time. O'Banion joined arms with the Torrio-Capone combine for the sally against Cicero and was given a liquor concession and a third interest in the Hawthorne Smoke Shop and its $50,0000 a day handbook.

O'Banion ruled the Gold Coast by means of his control over the votes in the neighborhood adjoining. He had been brought up in poverty, hustled papers, served as waiter in a notorious cafe and then turned to burglary and safe-blowing.

Three indictments in 1921 and one in 1922 had failed to hold out against his political influence and now he had a florist shop at 738 North State Street from which he operated the beer business that soon was to threaten the supremacy of the combine itself.

He loved flowers. He loved killing. He would have nothing to do with traffic in women and would not touch alcohol in any form. He was small and round-faced, limped with one leg and carried his head on one side. He was sometimes too bloody even for Torrio and Capone.

O'Banion's concession had been expected to produce $20,000 a month in Cicero but the canny "Deaney" had slipped a lot of his saloonkeeper friends into the place and soon grossed $100,000 a month with no cut for Capone or Torrio.

Torrio tried to make a new deal and was told to go "peddle his papers." Soon O'Banion's booze was getting more from Cicero than the Torrio-Capone beer got from the rest of the Chicago trade area. In gangland this would never do.

Trouble arose between O'Banion and the Six Sicilian Gennas whose alky-cookers furnished the raw material for the combine. The Gennas, willing killers, began edging into O'Banion territory. O'Banion pulled out of the combine and defied it with the all-inclusive insult "To hell with the Sicilians," which made it an inter-racial war.

It was war between O'Banion and the whole Torrio-Capone-Genna outfit. Election time came on and O'Banion was busy with the job of electing his friends and fighting the Gennas, not to mention any little skirmishes with Capone and Torrio.

Mike Merlo, founder and the only president of the Unione Sicilione to die a natural death, chose November 9, in that year of 1924, to perform his miraculous feat of passing out unmurdered.

I'VE told you already how O'Banion was given the quietus, in the famous glad hand murder.

After O'Banion was killed, officials made a pass at questioning Capone and Torrio.

Some have called O'Banion the "It" boy of gangland. Here he is with his bride in one of the few pictures he had taken while ruling the North Side gang. Dion carried three gats and a winning smile.

The business of questioning Capone was soon over. Torrio and the Gennas were also interviewed. John Scalise and Albert Anselmi, afterward to be called the Homicide Squad, were suspected but never tried. Frank Yale was believed to have been the third man, the handshaking killer.

Yale had done business before for Torrio when Capone was brought on from New York. Scalise and Anselmi were said to be imported from Europe by the Gennas.

Torrio and Capone attended the funeral. Then Capone went into retreat and Torrio fled with O'Banion men hot on his trail. They followed him from Hot Springs to New Orleans, to the Bahamas, to Cuba and back to Chicago and shot him down in front of his own house.

Torrio lived. But he did not remain long in Chicago.

Alphonse Capone took command of the combine.

Death had disrupted the Big Three. Death had scared out one of the Big Two.

Only the Big One remained, the Big Fellow, the Big Shot.

And Death's favorite son was he; Alphonse Capone.

Was he greater than these others, that he went forward where they fell or fled? There are some who believe he was. There are others who say his vision is not more active, his organizing ability not more extraordinary. These proclaim that he had the "guts," in gangland's own phrase, that his determination was matched by his nerve and his total lack of any compunction with regard to the methods he used to obtain the results he had in mind. That he selected the right men for his purpose is granted, that he played square with them is conceded, but that he has outstanding genius is still being questioned.

Taken for a ride in his own car, Peter Pulizzi is believed to have been slain by his passenger and to have died in the street as he leaped out the driver's door and tried to bring his own gun into action. It was found lying beside him where he fell in Chicago's West Side. The killer escaped.

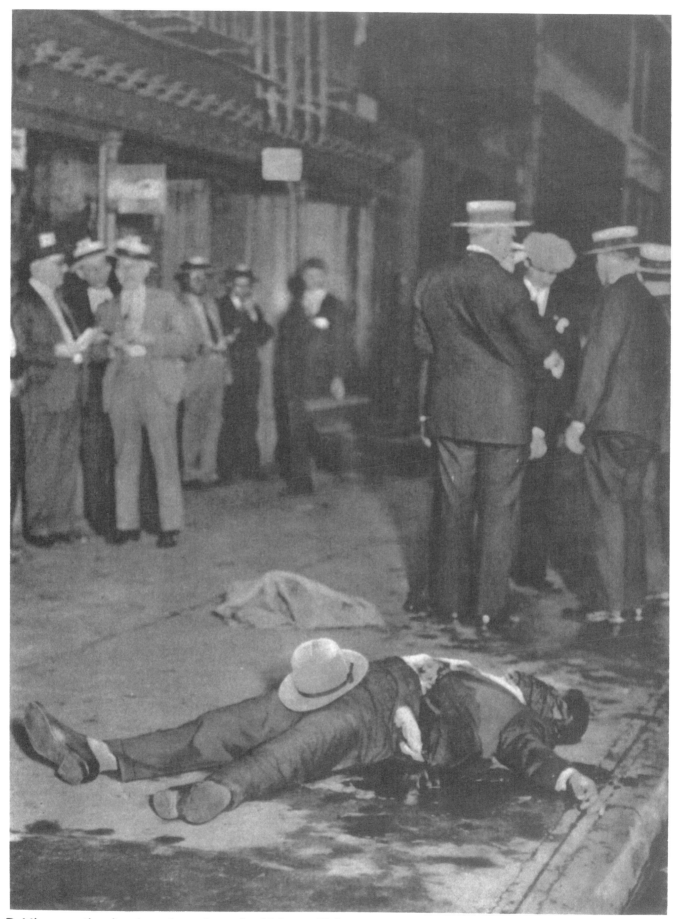

Public execution has been brought to its highest efficiency by gangdom. Here lies Giuseppe Micello, former convict, shot down by gangsters while 200 persons looked on. Calmly, as though they were unwatched, the murderers made their getaway at no unusual speed in their death car.

With a bodyguard at both elbows, Tony Lombardo walked down the crowded Chicago street—and gang guns roared.

A few moments later the Unione Sicilione was again without a president. Here's a close up of the top picture, with Lombardo the object of curious eyes. Tony had nevertheless served longer in the deadly president's chair than any of the others, and Al lost a good man the day Lombardo died.

Tony Lombardo as he looked at the height of his career as one of Al's favorites, and the head of the Sons of Sicily union

CHAPTER NINE: The Union of Death

UNEASY enough lies the head of the Chicago gang chief. But there is one throne more deadly and it is the command of this throne that makes Al Capone an emperor instead of a mere king.

For those who command kings are emperors and few kings are vested with such power as is placed in the hands of the president of the Unione Sicilione.

In union there is power. And in the Unione Sicilione is power doubled, redoubled, and tripled, for the sons of Sicily stick together, vote together, and kill together. Bear in mind that gangdom must be organized better than the Law is organized in order to succeed. It is done in rather simple fashion, by means of the Unions. Here are organizations ready made, with thousands of votes to cast for the politicians chosen by the presidents of the Unions. Without Unions, without prohibition and without guns—where would the gangsters be?

Al Capone is the emperor of gangland today and is likely to be tomorrow and up to Saturday night but such generalities as this cannot be safely made with regard to the kingship of the Sicilian Union.

Since the flight of Torrio and the accession of Capone to the Colosimo throne there have been six presidents of this association of the sons of Sicily. And now, no doubt, there is another one if he has not already gone the way of his predecessors. For the five men who mounted the fatal throne after the death of Mike Merlo have all died gangster deaths.

Two were slain in 1925. One served the better part of three years during which he was an ally of Capone's. And two more were killed in 1929.

What is the significance of the terrible fate that hangs over the presidency of this union of an immigrant race? What does this position which he would probably not accept, mean to Al Capone?

Empires are built upon kingdoms and upon the kingdom of the Unione Sicilione are the foundations of Capone's empire laid. For the Unione Sicilione is composed of 15,000 alky-cookers and supplies the raw material for Chicago's bootleg trade.

If you are a Sicilian and you live in Chicago, there is this opportunity open to you. Cast in your lot with the Unione Sicilione. Vote as its president commands. Set up your family in a tiny tenement somewhere and do as you are told. A still will be furnished you. Materials will be delivered at your door, usually the poisoned industrial alcohol of the prohibition law. Every day $15 will be placed in

While the battles for gang supremacy and the presidency of the all-powerful Unione Sicilione rage in Chicago, Al sits like a good general far behind the firing lines and decides what is to be done in the way of a nice killing or a new president.

your hand. Every day the product of your still will be taken away. And every day you will have an easy job, the job of tending the little still.

If you are molested, report the matter to the man who makes the daily visits. It will be well taken care of.

FROM the 15,000 alky-cookers' flats in Chicago comes the bulk of' the gin, the Bourbon, the Scotch and the other brands of high proof beverages that flow so freely in Chicago and its environs. These little stills are the washing pans with which the new gold rush pans its gold.

And so it is that the Unione Sicilione is important to Al Capone and to every other gang leader who aspires to control the liquor business in the vicinity of Chicago.

Angelo Genna of the Six Sicilian Gennas took the throne of this key kingdom on Merlo's death in November, 1924. He lived till May 26, 1925, when he was set upon by four men at Ogden and Hudson avenues and stopped four loads of shotgun slugs.

Until that time the Gennas were believed to have continued on friendly terms with Capone and his gang.

Samuel Amatuna, called Samoots, did not last much longer. He died of lead poisoning October 13, 1925.

In November, Alphonse Capone put Tony Lombardo on the throne of the Unione Sicilione. To Chicago's Italians and Sicilians he was the court of first and last resort. He dominated branches in St. Louis, Detroit, Pittsburgh, Cleveland, Philadelphia and New York.

Capone set out to keep Lombardo alive and Lombardo reciprocated by working hand in glove with Al. It was fair enough for the presidency he occupied was the coveted position in the world of Little Italy. In spite of its high percentage of fatality it was and still is the highest ambition of most of Chicago's Italians.

Lombardo ruled as a despot over the 15,000 Italians and Sicilians. Capone ruled Lombardo.

When Lombardo went out he was accompanied by

"Here's to your health, Lolardo," said his three friends, lifting glasses. With a smile the president of the Unione Sicilione raised his wine—and died. By the time his wife reached him the killers had fled.

Samoots Amatuna was president of the Death Union but not for long. Gang bullets ended his career.

a bodyguard composed of Joseph Lolordo and Joseph Ferraro. On the afternoon of September 7, 1928, the three went out together.

They walked half a block north on Dearborn Street to Madison, turned west in the thronged thoroughfare, Ferraro on the left and Lolordo on the right of Lombardo. Their hands were at the butts of their revolvers. At State and Madison they passed a restaurant.

The crowd was a crush. Two men fell in behind them as they made their way through the press. From the distance of a pace or two they fired. Lombardo fell with dumdum bullets in his brain. Ferraro, hit in the spine, lay paralyzed. Lolordo, unhurt, gave chase, revolver in hand.

Thirty feet away a brave policeman grabbed him, knocked his gun out of his hand, thrust his own gun into his belly and held him for the police car, convinced he had captured an assassin.

CAPONE hurried home from Florida for the funeral. He did not know, he said, who had killed Lombardo. Beside him, when he spoke, were Scalise and Anselmi, called his Homicide Squad.

He placed on Lombardo's throne, the older brother of one of his bodyguard, Pasqualino Lolordo. And Lolordo drank his toast to death on the eighth of the next January.

Two men waited for him and his wife when they came from a shopping trip that afternoon. They chatted for half an hour with Lolordo and left. Five minutes later her husband answered the door and three men entered. He welcomed them and set out food and drink. Then he closed the door of his living room.

Mrs. Lolordo heard voices and laughter. She heard at the end of an hour, someone proposing the toast, "Here's to Pasqualino." Then she heard shots instead of the clink of glasses.

Three men shoved her aside as she ran toward the door which had suddenly burst open. Her husband was dead.

Followed Lolordo on the throne of Little Italy, one Joseph Guinta, who had been brought from New York to help Tony Lombardo handle the affairs of the Unione Sicilione.

Guinta, too, went the route. On May 8, four months to the day after the previous president had died as his killers toasted his name, Guinta died in the same way.

There are those who tell a story of poetical justice in the passing of Joe Guinta. He sat, they say with those two cheerful boys called the Homicide Squad, Scalise and Anselmi. The three were being wined and dined by a group gathered for merriment. In the midst of it all guns roared, and the three men died.

And the story goes on to say that Guinta, Scalise, and Anselmi had been discovered making treacherous plots against their emperor, the chubby scar-faced one.

Joe Aiello succeeded Guinta and he, too, grew ambitious. He passed out over the same route Hymie Weiss had taken.

Anyway, the Unione Sicilione will have other presidents, and no doubt they will be selected by Alphonse Capone. And they, too, no doubt, will die the gangster's death which always overtakes the head of that organization—now called the Italo-American Union.

And but for the Italian wall of silence which causes the members of this race to die rather than reveal the names of those who bully or exploit them, the Union of Death would be just another business organization.

Davie Fuchs tried daylight banditry on Patrolman Harry Roth's beat in New York City. Roth got him in a running fight and is here shown on the extreme right with Sergeant Patrick Hearns as they stood beside the body of the slain holdup.

Chapter Ten: Kill or Be Killed

IT'S AN old jungle law that among killers, you must kill in order to live.

And the best man at the business end of a revolver, or the best at devising means of ridding himself of his enemies, is going to survive the longest in gangland.

That's one way of looking at Al Capone.

I think Al made up his mind that he would have to get out or else become supreme, way back when O'Banion was killed. Al chose the more dangerous path. He determined to climb to the top of the heap and stay there.

His partner, John Torrio, made a different decision.

You can almost see Johnny and Al talking it over after O'Banion's blood blended with the rose petals.

Johnny probably saw it first for he was the diplomat of the combination. Both of them were probably a little scared, for O'Banion had powerful followers and there was no fix for the O'Banion murder with O'Banion's men. Things might be arranged with the police who didn't care much anyway so long as one gangster killed off another. But the only way to halt reprisals by the other gang was to shoot fast and to shoot first.

The fact that the O'Banion followers went on Torrio's trail first indicates that the O'Banion men held the Torrio-Capone combination responsible for O'Banion's death. Somebody went after the Gennas later, but it was Torrio who drew the first pursuit.

Even before they caught up with him on January 24, 1925, a fleet of motor cars had shot up the Torrio-Capone headquarters in the Hawthorne Arms at Cicero. That was January 12 and the story goes that Capone dodged the bullets of that fusillade by lying flat on the floor in the restaurant that was riddled with gunfire.

Torrio in flight. Capone dodging bullets. Then Torrio sent to the hospital from which he left by a fire escape for a short prison term and then a trip to Europe. Capone in command at last.

Apparently Capone had decided to stick while Torrio took a run-out powder.

Then three Gennas died in May, June and July. Angelo Genna got it May 26, from four men with sawed-off shotguns and a car at Odgen and Hudson Avenue. Mike got it from the policeman who survived a chase and a clash when he was riding with Scalise and Anselmi. Tony Genna got it from three men as one of them shook hands with him at Curtis and Grand Avenue. The other three Gennas failed to fight back.

One story is that Mike Genna was being taken for a ride by Scalise and Anselmi when the police car overtook their machine and shot it out with them, killing the selected victim. The other angle is that Scalise and Anselmi were Genna killers brought in for the O'Banion job and others.

CAPONE has sometimes been blamed for the Genna murders, but it was Hymie Weiss, O'Banion's lieutenant, who shot up the Capone headquarters in Cicero with his fleet of cars. Weiss gunmen are almost certainly responsible for the attack on Torrio.

And there is as good reason for thinking that Weiss and his men got the Gennas as for believing that Capone had his killers out after these allies of his so soon after O'Banion's death.

Capone stayed and Capone prospered. The gangs that played the game with Capone lived and prospered. Those that tried to cut in on his territory or

Tony Genna died in the gang war. Some say Hymie Weiss killed him and some lay it to Capone.

to cut him down with machine gun, pistol or shotgun fire, did not live or prosper.

And yet how long it has been since Capone has been questioned about a killing! How long it has been since there was any real friction between Capone and the Chicago police! And how much has Capone contributed to the political funds of Big Bill Thompson and his crowd?

Some of those contributions are a matter of record. When Thompson went back into office, Capone headquarters moved at once from Cicero to downtown Chicago.

When a Chicago dry cleaner wanted protection from racketeers in his field he took Capone in as a partner and got protection.

When a Chicago police chief or a Chicago mayor wanted to keep the gang situation under control in Chicago, is it not possible that he got similar service by the same method if the partnership had not already been arranged?

Capone does not fear the police. Capone has five hundred men under arms. Capone has influence and power.

More than one political administration has made its peace with one faction of the underworld and given it the job of keeping the rest of the underworld under control.

For a Chicago political administration to make such a deal with Capone would mean a cut of his fabulous wealth and, perhaps his assurance that he would keep other gangsters and racketeers out, would keep his own men under a firm hand and prevent them from acts discreditable to the administration, and would be ready to fight for the administration at every election.

Big Bill Thompson may have resisted the temptation to play with such a combination of power. And then again he may not have resisted.

Perhaps Capone is Chicago's unofficial chief of police. Perhaps Capone's five hundred men under arms is the unofficial police force of Chicago.

And there are those who say that Capone is a greater force for law and order outside his own realms of law-breaking than any individual in the great city, that Chicago, like the laundry owner who made him a partner, has found the best and cheapest way to protect itself against the depredations of the gangs.

"Wally" Quinlan helped kill "Samoots" Amatuna. Here's what happened to Wally when gangsters caught up with him a little later in a saloon. This killing was chalked up for the Gennas.

"In the midst of peace there is war," originated, perhaps, in Chicago. So Dingbat O'Berta was doomed to take his last ride—but first he wedded the widow of Big Tim Murphy, and aspired to a high place in gangdom.

CHAPTER ELEVEN: Dingbat and the Dove of Peace

WITH the death of Hymie Weiss, Al Capone ruled supreme in the north. He was unopposed in the west. The south was his as far as Chicago Heights. Only Polack Joe Saltis opposed him on the great Southwest Side.

And Saltis had been his ally.

But the death of Weiss brought to light—from the pockets of the dead gangster—evidence that he had joined forces with Saltis to put Capone out of business.

Saltis and his bodyguard, Lefty Koncil, were on trial for the murder of Mitters Foley and Weiss had papers showing that he was working for their release. Dingbat O'Berta, who had been indicted with Saltis and Koncil had been granted a separate trial.

Saltis and his man were freed by a jury and O'Berta's case was stricken from the calendar. Saltis had nothing more to fear from the police at the moment but he had much to fear from Capone's men whom he had double crossed.

Green about the fat jowls, Saltis appealed to Dingbat O'Berta. O'Berta knew that brains were needed and sent for Maxie Eisen, a fish-market racketeer, who had the reputation of being even smarter than Jack Guzik who was admittedly the brains of Capone's crowd.

Maxie had returned from a trip around the world on the day of Weiss' death and was nervous on his own account. When Dingbat called on him for aid, he looked the situation over and announced that the war must be called off.

"You're all saps," he said, "killing each other off while the cops laugh. How about getting together?"

Saltis and O'Berta were eager. Schemer Drucci and Bugs Moran liked the idea. Myles and Klondike O'Donnell fell in with it. Let Maxie approach the big shot.

But Maxie didn't do that. He went to Tony Lombardo who ruled the Unione Sicilione and was a partner of Joseph Aiello. He knew Capone would listen to Lombardo and he knew that Lombardo would like the idea.

Maxie mentioned the subject casually, revealed that Moran and Drucci and the O'Donnells, even Saltis and O'Berta were sick of the killing business.

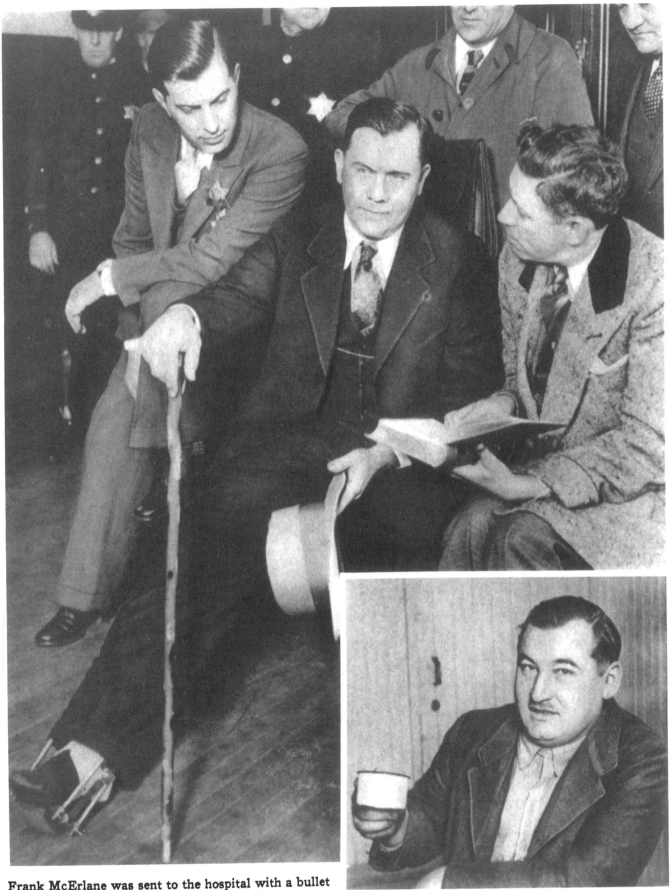

Frank McErlane was sent to the hospital with a bullet in his leg. While there some gangsters tried to pop him off. Frank wouldn't squeal, but he would say this: "You'll find them both in a ditch in a week or so!" And that's where they found Dingbat and his bodyguard.

Joe Saltis, big beer baron, drinking a cop o' "mud" in the Chicago hoosegow, where Joe went for refuge when things got too hot. He found peace in jail.

This is what they did to The Dingbat. He and his chauffeur-bodyguard, Sammy Malaga, died only a little while after Dingbat was blamed for taking a shot at Frank McErlane in the hospital.

Then he shifted to other topics of conversation.

Within another day or two Maxie Eisen was summoned to the presence. Capone wanted to see him.

The upshot of all this was that Maxie was to arrange a meeting which he did on October 20, 1926.

WITHOUT guns or bodyguards, Al Capone, by virtue of both the commander of a bootleg empire, entered a room in the Hotel Sherman across the street from the office of the chief of police and talked it over with his enemies.

There were in the room besides Capone, these other men: Antonio Lombardo, head of the Sicilian Union; Jack Guzik, business manager for Capone;

Ralph Sheldon, beer and alky peddler; Bugs Moran, ex-convict who was to loom larger presently; Schemer Drucci, whom the police were to kill in six months; William Skidmore, ex-saloonkeeper and court fixer; Barney Bertsche, yegg and peterman; and Jack Zuta, divekeeper.

Saltis and Koncil were still in jail and the O'Donnells had not got back their nerve since Duffy, Doherty and McSwiggin died.

For the treacherous gunner among these who had been able to smuggle a gun past the door might have awaited the command of all Chicago's liquor trade. But no one tried it. Maxie Eisen probably went over them all with the greatest care, even the big fellow.

59

"You'll find 'em in a ditch," McErlane had said and that may be the reason Sammy Malaga's body was thrown into the half frozen water into which O'Berta's car plunged with death at the wheel.

The gangsters who met here went at the business on a business basis. That Al was now the big shot was evidenced by the way his terms were agreed to. He dictated those terms and it is said of them that they were most generous.

The past was to be past. Everybody started from scratch. There were to be no more beatings, no more murders. Past killings were to be regarded as closed incidents. Incriminating documents of earlier date were to be disregarded even if they appeared. Leaders were to be held responsible for acts of their men and to discipline their own men.

Moran and Drucci were given the Forty-second and Forty-third Wards. Skidmore and Bertsche were told to see Al about future operations in the territory once held by Weiss and O'Banion. Saltis was ordered to stay southwest of Packingtown. The O'Donnells were not mentioned. Capone was to be supreme on the west from the Loop to Cicero, on the south to the Indiana boundary and down to Chicago Heights.

Maxie was satisfied. Saltis and Koncil and O'Berta were overjoyed and everybody else seemed pleased. All was quiet for two months. Then one of Ralph Sheldon's men was killed. Reprisals left Lefty Koncil and Big Hayes Hubacek dead in an auto ambush and Polack Joe Saltis moved very cautiously thereafter.

Another pose of the Dingbat and his wife. Mrs. O'Berta had a run of tough luck with her gangster husbands, losing first Big Tim Murphy and then Dingbat. A clever woman, she handled business matters for each of her husbands. Like O'Banion, the Dingbat used a flower shop as his front. Posies always appeal to the artistic souls of gangsters, and there's always money in the racket—think of the thousands of dollars spent for gang funerals! Some of 'em should try the undertaking business.

CHAPTER TWELVE: Aiello Challenges

AL CAPONE did not kill Schemer Drucci. The Schemer was knocked off in a hoodlum round-up by a young policeman from whom it is said he tried to take a gun with curses.

His attorney called it murder but the young policeman was praised. It has never been openly charged that the Chicago police were doing any of the retail killing necessary to the advancement of the Capone cause.

There seemed now to be little or nothing for Capone to worry about. Then Joe Aiello stepped into the picture. Joe had been a partner of Tony Lombardo in the cheese business but grew jealous of the latter when he was elevated to the kingship in the Unione Sicilione. He had upward of a dozen brothers and cousins, thus being the head of a Sicilian clan.

The Aiellos began their movement by organizing branches of the Unione outside Chicago which resulted in killings elsewhere, notably in St. Louis and Springfield, Ill.

Then they reorganized the old Genna mob and united with it Bugs Moran, Skidmore, Bertsche and Jack Zuta. Their next move was toward the assassination of the Emperor Capone and his prime minister, Lombardo.

It is said they offered a chef of the Little Italy cafe $10,000 to put prussic acid in Al's soup. Then they offered $50,000 to any gunman who could prove he had killed Capone.

Developments followed, but not the particular development they are said to have expected. Capone moved unscathed but four ambitious men from outside the city passed mysteriously out leaving considerable sums of money and jewels on their dead persons.

Jack McGurn, one of Capone's bright young men, was questioned for some reason. He was found at Capone headquarters.

McGurn was born James De Mora, the son of an Italian grocer, who was shot to death in front of his store in 1923. Jack, 19 when his father died, had been a promising boxer. He quit the ring and went out to avenge his father's death. Now it was said he was an expert machine gunner. Report gives him 22 notches on the handle of his Tommy gun. He was questioned.

The dead men had been identified as Antonio Torchio of New York, Anthony K. Russo and Vincent Spicuzza of St. Louis, and Samuel Valente of Cleveland.

Each of them had been found to hold in his hand after his death a bright nickel. It was all they were ever to win of the $50,000 reward for Capone dead and, though the report is credited in some quarters

that they were killed by Moran gangsters, there is more than a suspicion on the part of those who suppose they know that the nickels came from the unmeasured coffers of Al Capone.

Six members of the old Genna organization followed these, Lawrence La Presta, Diego Attlominonte, Numio Jamericco, Lorenzo Algano, Giovanni Blaudins, and Dominic Cinderella.

Still Capone was unscathed.

THEN followed a story unbelievable in its extravagance, but vouched for by Chicago authority. It may be called the siege of the detective bureau.

A machine gun nest had been found opposite Lombardo's home at 4442 Washington Boulevard. An-

James Belcastro, one of Chicago's public enemies, faced one of the famous "vag" charges with equanimity but he lost his aplomb when gangster bullets mowed him down—not quite fatally—only a few weeks ago.

The presidents of the Unione Sicilione die and the latest to do so is Joe Aiello who succeeded Joe Guinta and with control of the "alky cookers" made a threat against Capone. Capone men had made him yell for mercy at the time of the Siege of the Detective Bureau but he became bold again and so was marked for death.

He went into hiding in a friend's apartment and made preparations to flee the country. He had railroad tickets for the Mexican border and on the 23rd of October, 1930, he left the apartment for a taxicab.

Rat-a-tat-tat. Machine guns were spitting death at him from across the street. He was wounded but he turned to an alley dragging out his automatic as he ran. Just when he must have believed himself safe from the deadly gunners in front of the house another fusillade of machine gun fire roared out from another window.

He fell with 60 bullets in him.

The pictures show how it was done. Joe's dapper personality may be seen on the right and on the opposite page is what happened to a couple of Aiello men just after one of them had m u r d e r e d Marco Magnabosco. They were recognized in death by Herma Magnabosco, age 9.

other was found in the Loop across the way from Capone's favorite loafing place at Hinky Dink's cigar store, at 311 South Clark Street.

A clue sent the police to the Rex Hotel where Angelo La Mantio, 23, of Milwaukee, and four of the Aiello crowd were found. La Mantio admitted he had been hired to kill Capone and Lombardo and divulged the Capone ambuscade.

Aiello was brought in.

He had not been there an hour when somebody noticed half a dozen taxis on the opposite side of the street from the detective bureau discharging twenty-five men.

The watcher recognized Louis Campagnia.

"It's the Capone gang," he cried. The detective bureau had been surrounded.

Two officers rushed out and grabbed Campagnia, Frank Perry and Samuel Marcus of Capone's body-guard.

Two guns were taken from Campagnia and Perry but only one was found on Marcus. In a moment or two he whipped a second gun from the inside of his shirt but was overpowered before he could shoot his way out.

The three were put in a cell next to Aiello's and a policeman placed as eavesdropper.

Aiello recognized his killers. He begged for mercy.

"Mops" Volpe, above, is one of Capone's right hand gangmen. Three-fingered Jack White, at the left, was rated as one of the toughest gunmen of his time.

"Can't we fix it up?" he wanted to know. He asked for fifteen days to sell his house and leave town with his wife and baby.

The three men laughed.

"You started this," they told him, "you dirty rat, you're as good as dead."

The police escorted Aiello to a taxicab. He pleaded for police protection.

They let him get out of Chicago and he was gone for eighteen months—until Capone went to jail in Philadelphia.

A machine gun fusillade on the Aiello and Zuta headquarters sufficed to send the other members of that clan back into the territory assigned them under the peace of Maxie Eisen and Capone again was master 'till Aiello should rise again and go the way of Hymie Weiss.

Death had taken care of some of Capone's friends in Cicero who had been indicted in seventy-eight liquor cases on evidence given by John Costenora and Santa Calebron, a saloonkeeper and a bartender.

When the case came to trial it was discovered that Costenora and Celebron had been killed.

Then Capone announced he was leaving Chicago.

Two of Chicago's bomb dealers, "pineapple peddlers," as gangland calls them, are here seen cringing in the flare of a photographer's flashlight. They are Mike Casselli, left, and Steve Ficke, right, in the custody of Deputy Sheriff John Lynch, who has no reason to be afraid of the explosion.

Detectives have been looking for Sammy Stein since he killed "Happy" Smith, Kansas City traffic officer, in a bank holdup during the Republican Convention in 1928. They found him, riddled by gangster bullets on a road near White Bear Lake in Minnesota.

The grapevine of gangland s c o o p e d the news telegraph when S a m m y Stein (left above) "Weinie" C o l e m a n (right above) and Mike Rusick (below) were killed near White Bear. Chicago newspapers, tipped off by gangland, were asking for news of the killing many hours before the bodies had been found. Kansas City asked for the body of Frank Coleman before "Weinie" had been identified in a St. Paul hospital, if not actually before he died. Stein originally hailed from Minneapolis. Coleman and Rusick were Kansas City red hots.

The three, shortly before, had staged one of the most daring bank robberies in the history of the Northwest when they raided the Bank of Wilmar, Minn. They had been hiding out at a lake resort after cutting up $77,000.

Sammy Stein, the leader of the trio, was known in the vicinity as the "Ten Dollar Kid" because of the size of his tips. He was wanted for the murder of a traffic policeman in Kansas City. But more than that he was wanted by gangland for his habit of robbing his associates of their share in the robbery ventures in which they engaged. In the Home Trust Company robbery, following which the policeman was killed, the robbers got $19,000 and Stein is said to have double-crossed his pals and k e p t the whole amount.

Stein's body was found standing upright with one arm hooked over the limb of a small tree. His gun was in his hand but it hadn't been fired. Gangland had at last collected from Sammy Stein for the double-crosses he had worked.

Chapter Thirteen: The Vagabond Emperor

IT HAS been considered strange that Al Capone, when he had reduced to subjection every threatening element in the underworld of Chicago, should have wanted to leave.

But is it so strange?

There was never a man who enjoyed being a prisoner of his fate.

Al had killed to avoid being killed or had seen to it that death struck where he directed. His organization was all powerful, invincible. It would run itself. Al was ready to retire and leave the business to other men. He'd had enough.

The supreme test of his power would be to abdicate it. If Capone had reached the point where he could step out of active participation in his business, if he could go to some peaceful spot and live on his fortune the rest of his life, he would have proved himself the first man big enough to take an out after he'd been in.

Capone himself has said: "Once you're in there's no out." But apparently he wanted to test the truth of the statement.

He announced that he was shaking the dust of Chicago from his feet and didn't know when he'd be back, if ever.

For the first time, perhaps, in all his career he talked for publication. He lamented the reputation he had as a killer. His wife and mother, he said, had heard so much about him as a terrible criminal that it was too much for them. He was sick of it himself.

He told how a woman in England had tried to get him to cross the ocean and kill some neighbors.

He announced he was going to Florida and left December 10, 1927, with his wife, his son and a two-man bodyguard. But he did not go to Florida.

A few days later he turned up in Los Angeles with his presence there proclaimed through the newspapers. James E. Davis, chief of police, called on the Capone family.

"You're not wanted here," he told Capone. "You have twelve hours to go."

He was on a Santa Fe train December 14 headed east.

He complained that Los Angeles had failed in its welcome to tourists, that he had got the bum's rush when the newspapers gave him the front page and that somebody had stolen his wine.

"A swell dump," was his comment on Los Angeles.

And then Chief Hughes of the Chicago police announced that he couldn't come back to Chicago.

THE poor little rich gangster was out of luck. He tried to sidestep Hughes by getting off the train at Joliet. Chief John Corcoran there met the party,

Al Capone violates all the rules for gangster's dress. No checkered suits and loud vests for him! He wears neat straws, a fine watch chain, and modest ties.

took Capone and his bodyguard, disarmed them and charged them with carrying weapons. They were fined $2,601.

Capone stood on his legal right to enter Chicago. The chief backed his pronouncement by tailing him all over the place with uniformed coppers.

It was too much for Capone. He headed for Florida. St. Petersburg turned him out. Miami ordered him on his way. The colonial governor of the Bahamas barred him. New Orleans wouldn't let him stop there.

His efforts to find a home were ballyhoo for weeks. In the meantime a primary election was approaching in Chicago with the whole world notified that Capone had been ousted.

He had become an issue in Chicago and was doing his best not only to find a spot on which to alight but to relieve his Chicago friends of their embarrassment in having him there.

Finally, with the connivance of a broker, Capone bought his magnificent villa on Palm Island at Miami Beach.

There was a fight, but he stood on his rights as a property owner and defied Florida to oust him.

In the meantime, Diamond Joe Esposito, pictur-

Capone's Miami home is one of the show places
of the famous resort. No blood on these walls.

esque sheepherder of Deneen votes in Chicago passed
out by the shotgun route with none to say by whose
will he had died. The pineapple primary ended with
a licking for Big Bill Thompson and his cohorts.
Octavius C. Granady, negro ex-service man, Deneen
candidate against Morris Eller, was mowed down by
machine gun fire.

Capone, supposed to be in Florida, cast his vote
at his Chicago home and helped whip Cicero into line.
It was the America First campaign with Thompson
declaring war on King George of England but it was
a flop and the Deneen faction won by an overwhelm-
ing vote.

Thompson, still in the mayor's chair, refused to

resign as he had threatened to do. Chief Hughes
was sacrificed for the good of the cause and William
F. Russell, Jake Lingle's friend, was made chief of
police.

For the first time in years, the city of Chicago was
making a desperate fight to control its own des-
tinies.

A division had been called for. Those who would
not knuckle under to the gangsters had to stand up
and be counted.

It was a challenge to Capone and his ilk but the
Big Fellow gave it little heed. There was no need
for alarm as long as the illicit booze business was
good.

CHAPTER FOURTEEN: Gangster's Sanctuary

THERE has always seemed to be something phoney about Al Capone's sojourn in Eastern Penitentiary in Pennsylvania.

Yet, even a gangster king may want a vacation. Underworld emperors may grow weary of dodging pineapples, machine gun fusillades or deadly handshakes.

Even at Palm Island he was on the spot. He must maintain eternal vigilance if he were to sleep a night or live a day. Johnny Torrio had had a few months of respite behind prison walls. Johnny had a home in Italy he could go to for a few more months of practical obscurity.

But the Big Fellow had not where to lay his head in the secure knowledge that he would wake up in the morning.

Just what was back of the Pennsylvania rap, may never be known but he took a member of his bodyguard to the Eastern Penitentiary with him.

It is said there had been a new peace signed at the President Hotel in Atlantic City. It is said the suggestion had come from him. Capone had formed a new executive council to handle his business affairs. Johnny Torrio had come back to be the new chief of staff.

Then, his affairs in order, Scarface Al and his bodyguard, Slippery Frank Rio, came out of a motion picture theatre, stepped into the arms of a policeman and were arrested for carrying concealed weapons.

Facing Major L. B. Schofield, Philadelphia's director of Public Safety, the Big Fellow talked.

"I haven't had any peace of mind in years. I never know when I'm going to get it. I've got to hide from the rest of the racketeers and travel under an assumed name.

"I can't get away from the parasites that are always begging favors. I can't go anywhere without a bodyguard."

He declared he was tired of everything and would be the happiest man in the world if he could forget the gang murders and go to Palm Island and forget everything with his wife and his 11-year-old boy.

He wanted to live and let live. He wanted peace.

Questioned by the police, he said he had been arrested in Joliet for carrying concealed weapons but hadn't done any time.

Reminded of his New York record he admitted he had been picked up on suspicion of murder but discharged. He said he had once been arrested in Olean, New York, charged with disorderly conduct but had been discharged.

"I've never done a minute of time anywhere," he said proudly.

Within a few hours he was doing his first stretch.

He wasn't Al Capone any more. He was No. 90725 at the Holmesburg County jail and then he was transferred to Eastern Penitentiary, where things were easier, and became No. 5527-C.

THE STORY is that Capone expected a three-months vacation, but he drew a year.

At Eastern Penitentiary, Al had his own cell and

Frankie Yale ruled New York Sicilians and dealt with Al Capone, his old friend. When he double-crossed Al he had not long to live.

Capone's Chicago home at 7244 Prairie Avenue is nothing extraordinary. It is seen here under police guard. Cops waited for him to appear following his release from a Pennsylvania penitentiary, but Al didn't show. When he did he appeared at the detective bureau with his old query: "What you got on me, chief?"

the privilege of making long distance telephone calls. He was allowed to use the warden's office for business with his attorneys who then conferred with Al's brother, Ralph; with Jack Guzik, his business manager; Frank Nitti, his treasurer; and Mike Carozza.

Twice a month Johnny Torrio took a run up to Chicago by airplane and returned to the more peaceful confines of his home in Brooklyn.

In the meantime there was another masterpiece of murder that wrote the trademark of originality on the police records. This time it was the testimonial banquet murder and the victims were Joseph Guinta, the latest president of the Unione Sicilione, and the good old Homicide Squad, Scalise and Anselmi.

The story goes that these three had decided to go to work for themselves, that they had connived to take over the organization and had made some plans to put Capone out of the way.

Gangland's version of the denouement is that a testimonial dinner was arranged for the three, perhaps with the idea of persuading them to come into the open with their proposal and to dramatize their accession to power.

A roadhouse near Hammond, Ind., is said to have been the scene of the festivities. The guests of honor were seated at the head of the table, Guinta in the center and the heavy guns, Scalise and Anselmi, at his right and left hands.

Another toast of death, no doubt, was drunk. Here's to our guests of honor. Here's to Guinta, Scalise and Anselmi.

Suddenly three men stood behind them with clubs and beat them almost to insensibility, then the way was cleared, the guns were turned loose and they were slain in their places at the banquet table.

Scalise and Anselmi went back to Sicily in boxes. Guinta, the fifth president of the Unione Sicilione since Mike Merlo, went to the cemetery where the other four lay.

Meanwhile, Al was giving an impersonation of Santa Claus in Eastern Penitentiary.

HE WAS soon the hero of the other prisoners. He bought trinkets that the prisoners had made and sent them to friends all over the country. He sent $1,200 to a needy orphanage and at Christmas time he distributed presents to all of his prison mates.

He was kind, cheery and had no kick about anything. He worked in the files and was pronounced to have brains. He chatted on many subjects with

One by one the friends of Legs Diamond, sometimes called the C a p o n e of New York, are found like this. Joseph Hamley, a Diamond lieutenant, fell in a lonely road near Milburn, Newark, with six bullets in him.

the prison staff. His health was excellent. He gained eleven pounds in prison.

Newspapers quoted him on any and all subjects sometimes with and sometimes without the formality of interviews.

Back in Chicago, Frank McErlane was shot up in a hospital room and replied with a gun from under his pillow.

Asked who had attacked him by way of the fire escape, he said the folks would know in about two weeks.

Ten days later Dingbat O'Berta and his chauffeur, Sam Malaga, were taken for the gangland ride. The Dingbat was buried next to Big Tim Murphy whose widow he had married.

But these were ordinary killings, not the work of a master hand.

Capone was still in Eastern Penitentiary, but the best efforts of attorneys were being made to get him out. At the end of ten months he was freed.

Jake Lingle went to Philadelphia to get the big story of the release for the Chicago Tribune. Other correspondents thronged the prison yard.

Meantime, Capone had been slipped out and released from another prison. Jake Lingle missed him —or said he did. So did the other correspondents.

Capone's house at 7244 Prairie Avenue, Chicago, was surrounded day and night for three days after his release when no one knew where he was. But he didn't put in an appearance.

He popped up elsewhere and soon was back in his office which had been moved to the Lexington hotel.

With attorneys barring the police from molesting him, he laughed.

He declared he had never done anything but sell beer to the best people. His best customers, he said, were the ones who yelled loudest about him. Some of the judges used his stuff, as he revealed.

But Jake Lingle's death was to raise the biggest rumpus of them all.

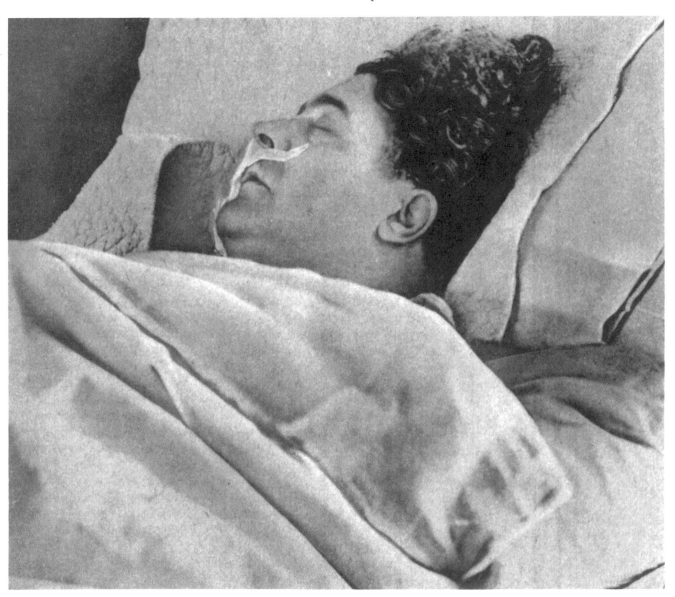

This friend of Legs Diamond isn't dead yet. He is Ritchie Boiardo, gang leader in his own right, and is here recovering from a bad attack of machine gun bullets.

Not only was Felix Le Presti killed but he was tortured and his tongue was slit beforehand, police found. His body is shown above where it was found.

Just another Chicago gangster on the spot. He is, or was, Pietro Porto until the pistols beat their rat-tat-tat as he left a cigar store and stepped into his car.

Chapter Fifteen: Jake Lingle

"GET THE MAN who killed Jake Lingle!" Colonel Robert R. McCormick, publisher of the *Chicago Tribune*, stood behind his desk in the Tribune Tower and faced Jack Boettiger across its glass top.

Boettiger, crack reporter on the paper that had hired the murdered "leg man," Lingle, stood with unchanged countenance, but an eager light shone in his eyes.

"Until the killer is dead or behind bars, you are to have no other business," the Colonel declared. "The Tribune will be behind you. GET LINGLE'S KILLER."

Boettiger reached a hand across the desk without a word and clutched that of Colonel McCormick. Then he took up the trail that led at last to the arrest of a man identified by nine persons as the actual murderer of the $65 a week crime reporter of the Tribune.

Chicago was in a furore. Lingle's body had scarcely been removed from the subway passage in which he had been shot down, when the Tribune had accepted as a challenge the death of its correspondent on the gang front and announced "enlistment for the duration" in its fight to bring the slayer to justice.

Boettiger's first move was to revisit the scene of the killing. He recreated bit by bit the action that had been played out there, the crime that blew things wide open in Chicago.

He worked out how the thing had happened before he took up the analysis that led him to the cor-rect solution. Here as he put it together little by little is the drama of the death of the Tribune re-porter.

Jake left his rooms in the Stevens Hotel about 10:30 that day, June 9, 1930. He made his way to the Tribune office. He visited in the local room where he had a desk. It was seldom used, since his duties took him to the haunts of the underworld and he reported generally by telephone.

After a little while he started toward the Loop. At a department store on State Street he bought a few things. Then he went to luncheon at the Sherman Hotel Coffee Shop where he had taken his noon-day meal for years.

Later he strolled in the lobby. Sergeant Thomas Alcock of the detective bureau saw him there and spoke to him.

"I'm being tailed," Lingle told him. Alcock looked around but could see no one. Jake moved to the cigar counter where he laid in a supply of cigars for the afternoon.

He was about to leave for the Washington Park race track and it was twenty minutes to train time. There was no hurry, though. The station was only four blocks away and he strolled that way in leisurely fashion.

It has since been revealed that Lingle had dodged what looked like a death car a few hours before. If he knew he was being followed as he had told Al-cock, it must have taken plenty of nerve for him to stroll that distance along Randolph Street.

The subway through which he was to pass from

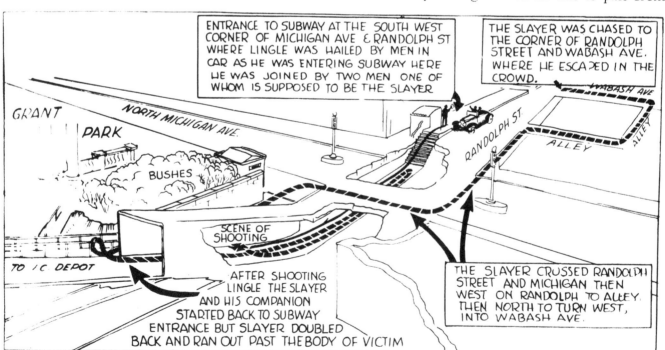

ENTRANCE TO SUBWAY AT THE SOUTH WEST CORNER OF MICHIGAN AVE & RANDOLPH ST WHERE LINGLE WAS HAILED BY MEN IN CAR AS HE WAS ENTERING SUBWAY HERE HE WAS JOINED BY TWO MEN ONE OF WHOM IS SUPPOSED TO BE THE SLAYER

THE SLAYER WAS CHASED TO THE CORNER OF RANDOLPH STREET AND WABASH AVE. WHERE HE ESCAPED IN THE CROWD.

AFTER SHOOTING LINGLE THE SLAYER AND HIS COMPANION STARTED BACK TO SUBWAY ENTRANCE BUT SLAYER DOUBLED BACK AND RAN OUT PAST THE BODY OF VICTIM

THE SLAYER CROSSED RANDOLPH STREET AND MICHIGAN THEN WEST ON RANDOLPH TO ALLEY, THEN NORTH TO TURN WEST, INTO WABASH AVE.

This map shows the vicinity of Lingle's death and the path of his slayer's escape. Lingle was on his way to the train which was to take him to his favorite racetrack when he was killed.

the Public Library to the Illinois Central Station in Grant Park must have seemed like a haven to him. If death was to come, surely it would be from a car somewhere in the stream of traffic that surged along Randolph.

He walked alone in the midst of the sidewalk throngs and must have listened for the crash of machine gun fire. But his steps did not falter, his nerve did not fail him.

Somewhere in that four blocks as he walked along, two men joined him in the crowd, seeming to fall in one at each side of him. He gave no sign he knew of their presence.

One was of light complexion, about five feet, ten inches tall and weighed around 160 pounds. He was about thirty years old, those who noticed him said. The other was not quite so tall, a dark man about 35, weighing 150 or so and dressed in dark blue.

AT THE entrance to the subway in front of the Library building is a news stand and, perhaps merely because he wanted it, perhaps to test whether the men walking beside him were covering him, Lingle halted here to buy a racing form. It was a natural action since he was on the way to the track.

Suddenly a small car, a roadster, whipped toward the curb out of the stream of traffic and drew abreast of him. If Lingle expected death, it must have taken all his nerve to hold himself under control as the machine slowed down.

Three men were in the car. Its horn sounded, plainly to attract Lingle's attention, a musical horn that caused him to look up.

One of the men leaned out of the car and hailed him.

"Play Hy Schneider in the third!" he called.

Lingle replied as though to a friend. He waved his hand. He smiled in recognition.

"I've got him," he shouted as the car moved on.

The cry of the men in the car has since been taken as the betrayal of the reporter. It may have meant anything. That it was not merely the friendly tip it appeared to be is indicated by the fact that no friend of his without cause to fear implication has come

John Boettiger, Chicago Tribune reporter, was told to get the killer of his fellow newspaper man and after six months of ceaseless work finally ran down the murderer, trapping Brothers as the man.

Margaret Farmer, Brothers' girl friend, gave police the slip when the slayer of Lingle was captured. She was taken later in St. Louis. She is also known as Margaret Walsh.

forward with the statement that it came from his lips.

It may have meant, "You have the right man." It may have meant, "Everything is set. Go ahead." It may have meant, "The coast is clear. None of his friends are about."

With the racing form held spread out before him, his cigar in his mouth, Lingle started down the steps that led into the subway. He was apparently engrossed in the racing "dope" in the paper. A friend passed him. Jake didn't see him.

He came to the bottom of the steps and crossed under the street. At the east end the subway exit is a ramp but a stairway comes down at one side from the east side of Randolph. Here the crowd was heavy.

The men who had been walking with Lingle had apparently gone on a little ahead. One—the dark man—stopped as if to buy a newspaper at a news stand beside the stairs. The light complexioned man stopped as though waiting for him.

As the latter turned he thrust a short-barreled belly gun at the back of Lingle's neck and pulled the trigger. The bullet crashed into Jake's brain and he pitched forward in a heap. His cigar was still in his mouth. The racing form was still clutched in his hand.

One man ran west. The other darted east out through the ramp, hurdled a fence and turned across Michigan Avenue. This man disappeared into an alley.

Someone yelled, "Get that man." A policeman turned and raced after him. The glove dropped by the fugitive was picked up. It was for the left hand.

BOETTIGER estimated there must have been from six to ten men stationed in the subway to cover that getaway. The killing had been perfectly organized both for the crime and the escape. At first it seemed to me to bear the earmarks of a Capone job.

But Boettiger would jump at no conclusions.

"The first thing to do," he said, "is to find out *why* Jake was killed. When we've got the motive we'll have something to work from."

They say Colonel McCormick raged when he first heard of the Lingle killing but it was nothing to the way he must have acted when the full story of Jake

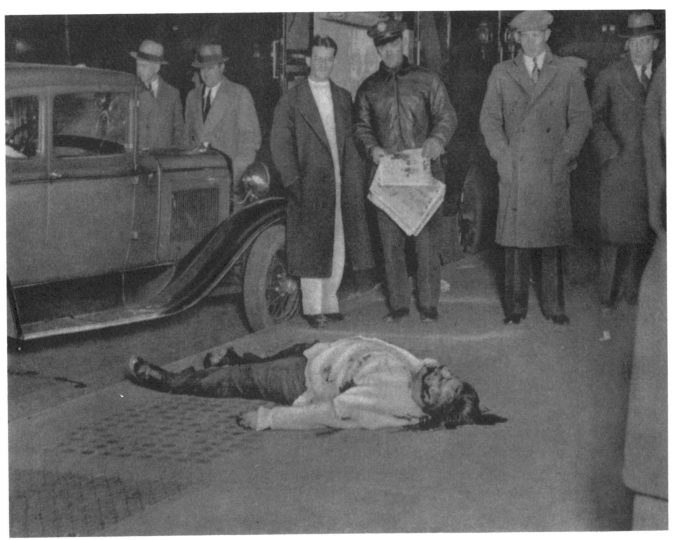

Red lights mean danger for gangmen. Natale Durso stopped his Ford at a traffic signal and he was riddled with bullets from another car that pulled up beside him and sped away.

The only time they ever put a number on Al Capone! He was Number 90725 at the Pennsylvania Pen, but to the world at large he is still Scarface Al, King of Gangland.

Jack Zuta had only a few more months to live when this picture was taken. He is the vice lord blamed by Capone men for Lingle's death. His taking off leaves only "Bugs" Moran of the n o t o r i o u s Zuta-Aiello-Moran combination. He dropped in a nickel and the machine guns played.

Lingle began to come in. The Tribune announced that it accepted the challenge of gangland but that was before the truth about Lingle had become known.

The real blowoff, I think, came when McCormick discovered that gangland had thrust its tentacles into his newspaper—that Lingle, known as the friend of Capone and of Police Commissioner William Russell, had for years been handling vast sums of money that could be explained only as of gang origin.

The Tribune found that Lingle had been spending $65,000 a year with a salary of $65 a week; it found that he and Russell had a joint trading account on the stock market and had lost huge sums in the market crash; it found the world credited Lingle with having placed Russell at the head of the police department and that he had been named in the street as the unofficial chief of police.

When the extent of Lingle's ramifications in the underworld and officialdom of Chicago became known, finding his killer seemed to be a hopeless proposition. To follow all the tangled skeins was impossible.

Who had killed him?

Was it the Capone execution squad? Or the work of Capone's rivals?

Alphonse Capone soon settled that question in his own inimitable way. A series of killings began to occur that showed who was responsible. The one sure way for finding out who killed a man is to wait and see what the dead man's friends do. Moreover, certain transactions of Lingle's that preceded his death indicated what had happened to put him on the spot.

Bit by bit, Boettiger learned that Lingle had tried a "fix" job for Zuta and his partners. He learned that Jake Lingle had taken $25,000 from Jack Zuta to grease the way for dog racing at the Chicago stadium.

But the fix didn't work. Dog racing was blocked by the courts and Zuta demanded return of the $25,000. The money had been spent in Jake's efforts. When Zuta wanted it back, Jake could get together only $9,000.

Some of this he borrowed. The agent who made Zuta's demand turned nasty. The day before the murder a demonstration with a death car had been made while Lingle talked to a friend in the street. There had been no shots but Lingle knew why the car drew near him. If he didn't raise the money, death would strike.

Then came chances to get the money together. The Sheridan Wave Club planned to open for gambling. Lingle was desperate for funds, and he offered to fix it up for half the profits.

The Biltmore Athletic Club wanted to open up in Aiello territory. Lingle is said to have told them they could operate and to have been about to collect $15,000 when Pat Roche of the state's attorney's office raided the place.

Another shot of Elegant Al Capone as he looks today.

Lingle tried to call Roche. Roche refused to answer the 'phone. Meeting the reporter the next day, he asked what the call was about.

"You have put me in a terrible jam," Lingle is quoted as saying. "I told that Biltmore outfit they could run!"

AND SO Lingle's chance to raise the rest of the $25,000 that might have saved his life was gone. And Pat Roche had had a hand in it by the raid on the Biltmore Club.

At last the Tribune investigator had the motive for the killing of Jake Lingle.

Jake had failed to produce results for Zuta and put across the dog racing. He had failed the Aiello interests when they wanted things fixed up so they could run their Biltmore Athletic Club.

That's why Jake was put on the spot.

Of course, proving that this was the reason would be difficult. The Zuta and Aiello interests were powerful.

There again gangdom showed that it dispenses

justice more swiftly than organized law. Al Capone knew who bumped off his friend Lingle. He had the lowdown on the case long before police or Tribune men could find out. That was indicated by what happened next.

Jack Zuta soon learned that the finger was on him. He narrowly escaped a bullet after leaving the detective bureau where he had been questioned on Lingle's killing. Jack knew that Al had him spotted as responsible for Jake's death, and took it on the lam. He wound up way over in Delafield, Wisconsin, to lie under cover at a summer resort. One fine day the Capone squad caught up with him. Zuta was putting nickels in the music box when machine guns blared, and he died with their music in his ears.

Joe Aiello went the route when a typical Capone machine gun ambush ripped him to pieces as he was getting ready to skip the country to safety.

Jake Lingle was avenged. But the actual killer was still at large.

Boettiger realized that any moment might bring the gang bullets about the head of the real killer, the man who had stepped up behind Jake and put the bullet into his brain. He was convined this man had not yet been found either by the police or by Capone.

Boettiger had avoided the police for the most part and worked with Roche and the state's attorney. But

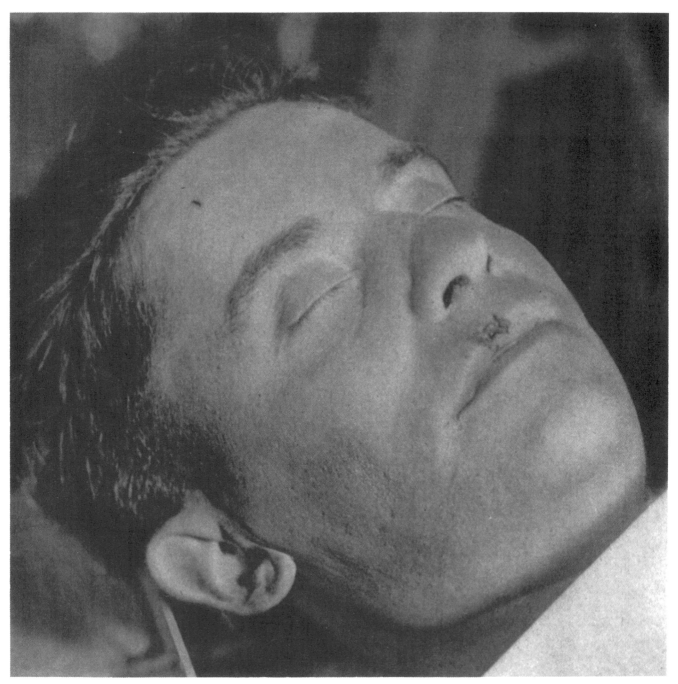

The power and glory of gangland don't mean much to Jack Zuta here. At the morgue all men are equal and Al Capone, though he may have had nothing to do with putting him there, may rest e a s i e r now that the smart Jewish vice leader is no more.

they seemed to be up against a blank wall. Most of the picture had cleared up but the view of the actual killer was still blurred. Nobody seemed to know who he was. His name had apparently not been mentioned in Chicago gangland.

This was logical, Boettiger believed. It was no new thing for a Chicago gang to import outside guns for a job like that.

It was a race to see who could put the finger on the slayer first. Again and again Boettiger was afraid he had been beaten to it. But rumor persisted that the man who had actually fired the murder gun was still at large.

Then came the tip-off that has raised a new question in gangland. Did Capone join forces with Boettiger and the state's attorney to bring the killer of his friend to book?

If so, was it a confession that Capone resources were not sufficient to turn up the man, or was it merely a courtesy of Capone's to give the actual murderer to the state's attorney and the Tribune while he took care of the big shots?

For the tip-off came from Capone sources. Mafalda, Al's sister, was being married to a brother of Frank Diamond, Capone lieutenant. Chicago was still so "hot" that Al couldn't attend the wedding. The wedding party, after some interference by the police, wound up at the Cotton Club in Cicero, owned by Ralph Capone.

Fred Burke, shown at the upper left, is said to be the most wanted man in America. He was sought after the Lingle killing, nearly captured, but made his escape. Danny Stanton, the gentleman with the white hat, is one of the listed public enemies of Chicago. He is said to have been for years a district commander for Capone. He is now fighting extradition in the case of the murder of Jack Zuta in Delafield, Wis.

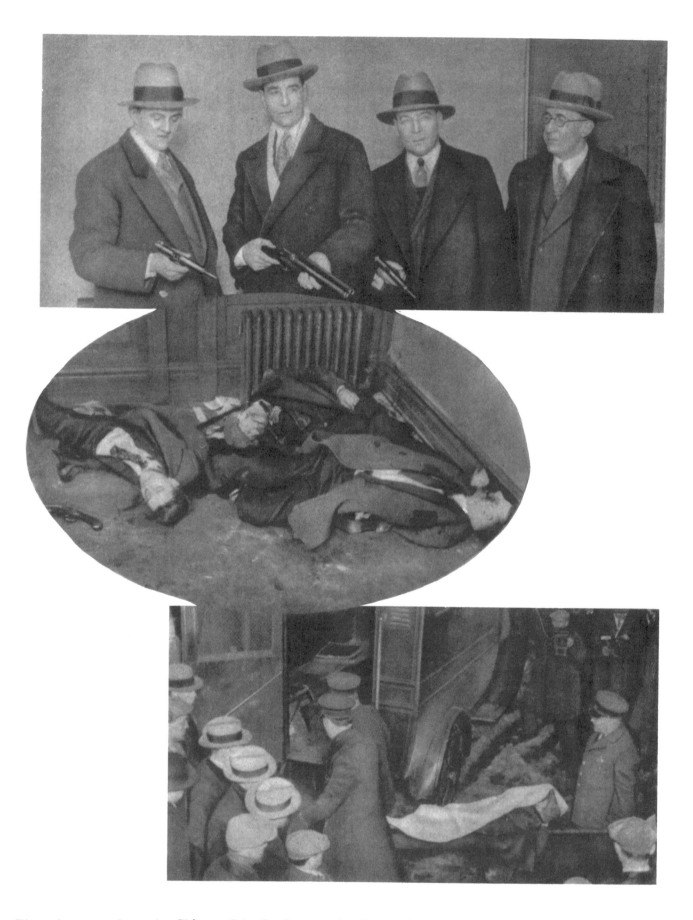

These four men from the Chicago detective bureau shot it out with racketeers trying to muscle in on the Tire Workers and Vulcanizers' Union. Bodies of "Dinky" Quan, William Wilson and William Ryan lay huddled in their own blood in a corner of the union office when the detective squad c o r n e r e d them.

Aviators flying near the Aviation Country club at Hicksville, Long Island, discovered the body of a gangster lying in an open field after his "ride."

Pat Roche was there with several of his men. Boettiger was with him and sat at the table beside him when a Capone gangster approached them.

"Can't you ever leave us alone, even on a night like this?" he asked.

"I'm holding down my job," Roche replied, "and that job is to find out who killed Lingle."

"Yeah?" the gangster sneered. "What would you do if you knew?"

There followed some whispered words. A few days later Boettiger and Roche were on the trail of Leo Brothers, a St. Louis gangster, whose name had never been mentioned in connection with the case.

THEY WENT after him cautiously. The whole story has not yet been told at this writing but, roughly, it is this: By Roche and Boettiger and their agents, Brothers' trail was followed through many cities and back to a hideout in Chicago. Once he was reported seen. The investigators held back, taking no chances of bungling the catch or running into another killing.

Bit, by bit, inch by inch, the net was drawn in about him. The man was not alarmed. Once it was feared he had been given the tipoff. It was reported he would leave on a certain train for St. Louis. Quick action followed. Detectives swooped down on the berth he was supposed to have. It yielded another man.

Then word came from Miss Rose Huebsch, formerly of Roche's office, that she had a room across from Brothers' in an apartment building and that a telephone call would bring him out of the room, there being no private phones.

The trap was carefully laid. Rose Huebsch went out to make the call. Boettiger and Roche's men hid in her room.

They waited most of one night. Before the dawn began to streak the east, he was seen to enter the building. A man who knew him flashed the signal to Rose Huebsch some distance away. The men waiting in Rose's room were tipped off.

Footsteps came along the hall. A key clicked in the lock across the way and the men knew where their quarry was.

Tense moments followed. They wanted to give him time so he would undress and lay aside his guns. Presently the ring of a telephone bell sounded through the quiet hall.

The voice of someone answered it. More footsteps. A knock. The voice of the suspected murderer.

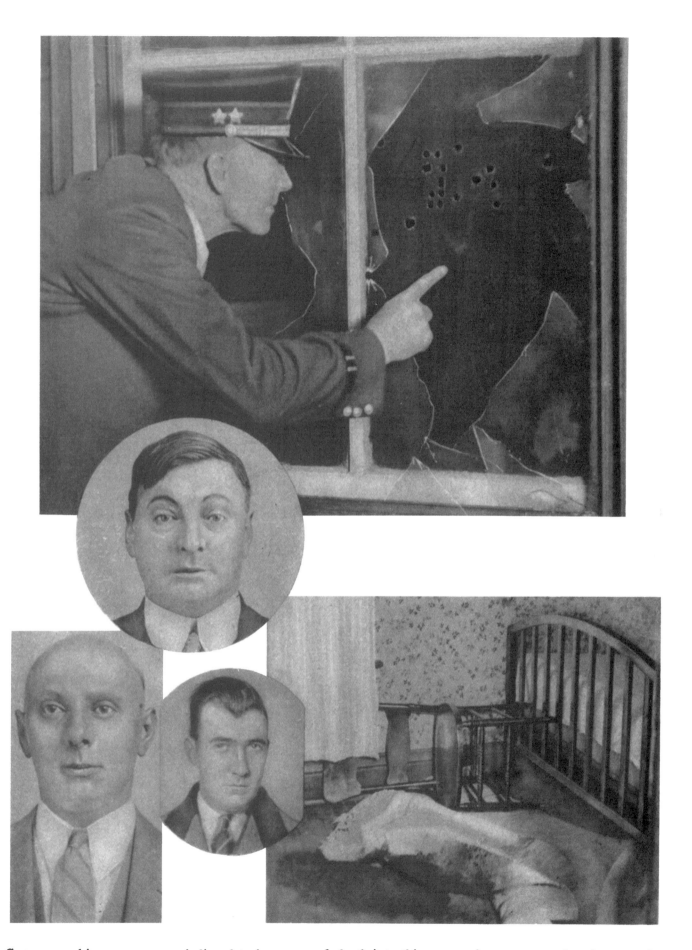

Capone machine gunners are believed to have poured death into this group of gangsters and racketeers when they got together in a Fox Lake resort planning to take the empire of gangdom from the warring cohorts of Moran and Scarface Al. Sam Pellar, Joe Bertsche and Michael Quirk died in the fusillade.

A car draws alongside the fine sedan of the gangster who is on the spot, guns roar suddenly, and—that's that. Here's a New York mobman, one Big Tom Sabatino, after taking a death ride. Just for the fun of it detectives are taking fingerprints. But killers are never brought to justice.

"What is it?" a sleepy voice, as though the suspect had already dropped off to sleep.

"Telephone." The footsteps went back the way they had come. A pause. The creaking of a bed. Another pause. Would the man arm himself before he came out the door? Then the click of the lock and the latch.

The soft footsteps of slippered feet. Rose's door was flung open with the sudden command:

"Up with your hands. We want you!"

The bathrobed figure stood there in pajamas and slippers in the dimly lighted hall. What light there was gleamed on the guns of Roche's men. Leo Brothers was captured without the firing of a shot, the man whom Pat Roche declared later was the "hardest mug" he had ever talked with.

"He hasn't a nerve in his body," he told the newspaper men after better than two weeks during which the arrest was kept secret.

Days followed days of questioning. Brothers stood up under it all. His record in St. Louis showed he had been arrested fifty or sixty times as a gangster and labor terrorist but had never been convicted. He answered perfectly the description of the Lingle killer. Nine persons, one by one, picked him out of groups as the man they had seen fire the fatal shot.

In Chicago he was known as Louis "Buster" Bader. He had fled there from St. Louis where he was wanted for a murder committed in 1929. He was 31 years old, had chestnut hair and was of good appearance. He said he was born in Belleville, Ill. It was found he had served on a submarine chaser during the World War.

And now at last there rises from the welter of crime in Chicago a new question. Will the Lingle killer talk?

Will Brothers, on his way to the chair, put the finger on the gangs? Can he put the finger on Capone? Is Al's throne tottering?

Al Capone is on the spot, put there by the worldwide notoriety his gangland activities have brought him. Perhaps he is on the spot in a more definite sense. Perhaps there is already in the hands of Jack Boettiger and Pat Roche the evidence that will send him to the chair along with the killer of his friend, Jake Lingle.

Who knows?

The first woman taken for a ride by gangland is covered by the blanket in the upper picture. She died in a lonely road near Boston. Below, side by side in death, lie Tony Calterone and Salvatore Tarolino, believed to have been shot down in the war over territorial rights among Brooklyn gangsters.

Gangland is hard on automobiles. Above is the car in which Philip Gnolfo, alky peddler and extortionist of Chicago's Little Italy, was slain with machine guns. Below is a car found at Maywood, Ill., after being dynamited. It is believed to be the getaway car used after the St. Valentine Massacre.

Somewhere today, if death has not overtaken him, Scarface Al Capone is "on the spot" with only his body-guard, headed by Frankie Rio (upper right) to stave off the inevitable end of the gangster chief. The peace of his Palm Island home (lower picture) will not be his for long.

EPILOGUE

Alphonse Capone was not a native of Chicago. He was a 21 year old dishwasher in a Brooklyn NY cabaret when the 18th Ammendment (Prohibition) took effect in 1920. His cousin, John Torrio, had gone to Chicago to run the outlaw enterprises of an uncle, Big Jim Colosimo, and he had Capone come West as his assistant. Torrio was called the "father of American gangsterdom" by a U.S. Treasury official and a British newspaper dubbed Capone "the 19th Ammendment.".

Capone, who served with the U.S. Army in France during WWI, had an income estimated at $30 million per year by the late 1920s. In a few short years he had consolidated his hold on the city of Chicago and was firmly in control of virtually every illegal activity.

In the wake of the particularly brutal "Pineapple Primary" elections (so called because of many bombings) in the Spring of 1928, Frank Loesch, a 75 year old founding member of the Chicago Crime Commission, paid Capone a visit. He sought Capone's help in insuring a free and honest general election in the Autumn. The election took place without incident.

Of greater historical interest is Loesch's description of his visit to Capone's headquarters in a suite of 6 rooms on the 4th floor of the Hotel Lexington near what is now McCormick Place. The bountiful lobby of the Lexington was heavily patrolled by Capone men who stayed in touch with his staff by phone. As one approached the nerve center of Capone's activities in Salon 430, he had to pass sentries and rows of bodyguards armed with .45 caliber pistols in shoulder holsters. In an oval vestibule a crest in the oak parquet flooring enclosed the initials AC. On the left was a bathroom of nile blue and royal purple ceramic tile containing an immense sunken tub with gold fixtures.

Capone at 29 looked old; the mountains of pasta and Niagaras of Chianti had left him fat. He stood 5 feet 10-½ inches tall and weighed 255 pounds. His hair was dark brown, his eyes light grey. A scar ran across his left cheek from the ear to the jaw, a second across the jaw and a third below his left ear.

As Capone was a late riser, visitors calling before noon often found him in a dressing gown and silk pajamas from Sulka, in royal blue with gold piping. A flawless 11-½ carat blue-white diamond adorned the middle finger of his right hand. He usually seated himself at a long mahogany desk with his back to the bay window, a cigar clenched between his teeth.

Shortly after Loesch's meeting with Capone the U.S. Supreme Court ruled that illegal income was to be considered taxable like all other income. Acting on the explicit orders of President Hoover, the Treasury Department successfully prosecuted Capone for tax evasion. He was sentenced on 24 October 1932 to 11 years in federal prison. He was released from Alcatraz on good behavior in 1939, suffering from a terminal case of neurosyphilis. He died from it on 25 January 1947.

CHICAGO IN THE 1980s

Capone's former home(left) at 7244 Prairie Avenue on the south side of Chicago still looks just as it did in the late 1920s. Compare with the photo on page 72.

The Lexington Hotel near MacCormick Place (below) retains none of its former elegance. It was renamed the New Michigan Hotel after the Capone era and has now stood empty for many years. Its furture is uncertain - restoration or destruction?

The site of Big Jim Colosimo's night club at 2126 South Wabash (above) is now a vacant lot in the slums of Chicago's near south side.

The lower photo was taken from the same spot as the one on page 24. The warehouse in which the St. Valentine's massacre occurred is now gone, replaced by a parking lot. The alley west of 2122 Clark Street is perfectly peaceful and no one could possibly imagine the horrors that took place there 60 years ago.

Capone, in G-Men Custody, Quakes as 'Freedom' Nears

LOS ANGELES —(U.P)— Alfonse (Scarface Al) Capone, brewer of some of the vilest concoctions that ever seared the innards of prohibition era drinkers, was in jowl-quaking fear for his life today on the eve of his release from Federal custody.

The Federal government also was worried. It made of his leave-taking from prison a mystery it hoped could not be solved by the trigger men, whom Capone swore were waiting to "rub him out" with erasers of lead.

G-men were in charge of him somewhere in the United States. That was all the Department of Justice would say. He was not scheduled to be released from his ten-year income tax sentence until next Sunday, nor will he be, but the Federal agents aren't saying where they'll do the releasing. He still may be in Terminal Island prison, in Los Angeles harbor, where he served the last ten months of his term. He may be en route to his white-walled castle in Miami Beach, Fla., or he may be in a hotel room in any of a dozen cities.

If he has left the prison, there wouldn't seem to be much chance of anyone recognizing him on the street.

Partly paralyzed from paresis, crinkly-skinned from loss of weight, totally bald and sometimes talking gibberish, Capone is a human caricature of Public Enemy No. 1, the man who took care of competition with machine guns. ..

Scarface Al went to prison—Atlanta, then Alcatraz—and he got time off for good behavior. Prohibition was repealed, and his lawyers spent their time digging up his fine. They paid it in installments, last of which they handed over only a few days ago. Capone still is reputed to be a millionaire several times over.

(F

U.S. Agents Keep Capone Vigil

BALTIMORE—(A')—Broken, flabby and ailing "Scarface" Al Capone stared vacantly at the ceiling of a $30 a day hospital suite today, free of prison cells in which he lived for seven years but sentenced now to a lingering brain disease.

Outside the one-time Chicago gang czar's room sat a male orderly and a nurse. In or near the hospital were three Federal agents, assigned by Attorney General Murphy to keep the fallen vice emperor under surveillance because, Murphy said, "certain things have come to our attention."

Whether the agents were to guard Capone from himself or from possible gangland reprisal was not made clear. No uniformed police were assigned to Union Memorial hospital and officials asserted none would be unless requested by the institution.

The gangster chief came here secretly Thursday from the Federal prison at Lewisburg, Pa., and entered the General hospital as the patient of Dr. Joseph E. Moore, former director of the syphilis division of the Johns Hopkins medical clinic.

He was suffering from paresis—softening of the brain—but it was learned that, while his condition is serious, he is in no immediate danger.

Attorney General Murphy said Capone would be under treatment, possibly three weeks, and planned to go to Miami after his discharge. Murphy added that relatives had assured him the racketeer, who served his time for income tax evasion, would "go straight."